# REBELLION

# REBELLION

## THE EPIC SAGA
OF
MARRIAGE, SATAN, AND THE BATTLE FOR OUR SOULS

by
Michael A. LaMorte

CATHOLIC TREEHOUSE, COLUMBUS, OHIO 2022

Published by Catholic Treehouse, Columbus, Ohio
www.catholictreehouse.com

*With endless gratitude to God for the talents He has entrusted to me and for the amazing wife He has so graciously blessed me with.*

*Dedicated to St. Michael the Archangel, who was first to fight Satan's rebellion against the Most High.*

*"As the family goes, so goes the nation
and so goes the whole world in which we live."*

SAINT JOHN PAUL II

# TABLE OF CONTENTS

# TABLE OF CONTENTS

*"Sin is an easy thing to us; we think little of it; we do not understand how the Creator can think much of it; we cannot bring our imagination to believe that it deserves retribution, and, when even in this world punishments follow upon it, we explain them away or turn our minds from them.*

*But consider what sin is in itself; it is rebellion against God."*

S T. J O H N  H E N R Y  N E W M A N

# AUTHOR'S NOTE

**GOD IS TRUTH.**

Love of God, therefore, is love of truth.

Searching for truth, therefore, is searching for God.

When I set out to write this book, I set out in search of truth to answer a question: how did we as a society get here, with regard to the state of marriage? How did it come to be that marriage—on both the individual level and as an institution—is attacked? And why? And who was responsible? I wanted to know what happened to cause the failure of so many marriages and I wanted to know when it started. I didn't know what a daunting task answering these questions would be.

As with any question someone has in this day and age, I started out with an internet search and assumed that the all-knowing search engines would return to me hundreds of thousands of potential answers in the twinkle of an eye. I was disappointed. They returned many results, mind you, but there was nothing even resembling an answer to my question. So I revised my search terms and searched again. And again, I was disappointed. Over and over I kept searching to no avail. So I began to investigate more.

I started with recent events and people. I looked at what influenced them. Okay, now we're getting somewhere. But then I looked at what influenced them. The story kept going back further. First twenty years, then fifty, then a hundred, then five hundred. And what I came to realize is that the current events are indeed attacks on marriage, but more importantly, they are all pivotal battles in an ages-long war between good and evil. What's more, we are still in the middle of fighting in this epic battle.

As I researched, I uncovered a lot of things I had never expected. Over and over, I continued to be surprised by truth. Some things that I had long held to be fiction were in fact truth; some things that I had believed to be truth were in fact fiction; other things that I long considered to be of minor significance turned out to be of major importance, and vice versa.

There were times I would run across something that I really wanted to use, but investigation proved it to be a fabrication or of questionable authenticity. Other times, there were truths that, quite frankly, I would rather have left out, but doing so would have been disingenuous. In the end, I endeavored to tell the whole story, following the truth wherever it led, and following the Holy Spirit wherever He led me.

Be prepared, however: *Rebellion* is not your typical Christian book, where at the climax, Christ on Calvary wins the victory, and we all go to Heaven. *Rebellion* is a story of a battle that is *still in progress.* While Christ died once for all, His final victory still awaits us. Until that day, we are still in the middle of a great war: the war for souls. The battle against marriage is the key battle in that war, and the attacks against marriage will never cease until Christ's final victory. *Rebellion* isn't a story of Christ's victory; rather, it is a wake-up call as well as a call to arms.

May you never tire of searching for truth, and love it when you find it.

May the truths herein illuminate your life.

*Onward, Christian soldiers.*

— Michael A. LaMorte, 18 November, 2021

# INTRODUCTION

M ARRIAGE is so fundamental to the foundation of society that Pope Paul VI in *Lumen Gentium* called marriage and the family the "Domestic Church," the smallest unit of faith. The Domestic Church is led by parents whose role is to "by their word and example, be the first preachers of the faith to their children." Therefore, the primary duty and responsibility of parents in every Domestic Church is to ensure that the souls of their children get to Heaven. Raising saints is their primary job, indeed it is their *vocation*. Yet it is beyond argument that as more and more people join the ranks of the "nones"—people who claim no religious affiliation—more and more souls are *not* making it to Heaven, where they were designed to be, (and where parents have a responsibility to get them.)

For thousands of years, marriage stood as the one unshakable, immovable foundation of society where husbands and wives died to themselves for the sake of their respective spouses and children. Divorce, separation, cohabitation, and children born out of wedlock were not just rare, they were cause for scandal. Yet in the past fifty years, all of these things have become increasingly normal parts of everyday life. No one is shocked anymore when a teenage girl becomes pregnant. There is no sense of shame when a married couple files for divorce. And when an unmarried couple decides to move in together, it's often a time of celebration among their family and friends. Instead of dying to self, everything has become about putting oneself first in everything, to the point of ending a marriage to be able to put oneself first. As one op-ed columnist wrote recently, "I divorced my husband not because I didn't love him. I divorced him because I loved myself more."[1] Even the very definition of marriage is under scrutiny and redefined seemingly every day.

Some see the changes as simply the long overdue modernization of society, mankind's enlightened evolution away from an inflexible and oppressive patriarchal scheme. Yet there is no end of research and data that shows that all of these situations—divorce, cohabitation, children raised by unwed single parents or same-sex couples—lead to poor outcomes for children, and generally unhappier people. And children who grow up in homes that are broken or non-traditional generally grow up to repeat these patterns in their own lives. A quick search on the internet will yield countless jaw-dropping statistics and head-shaking articles on these and related topics. "Single Parenthood And Poverty, The Undeniable Connection," one headline declares.[2] "One-third of girls whose fathers left the home before they turned 6 ended up pregnant as teenagers,"[3] another article tells us. "Children whose parents divorce are, on average, less likely to complete high school and attend and complete college," found another.[4] And on, and on, and on....

With marriage destabilized, it cannot be questioned that our society, now moved away from its very foundation, has become unsound on many levels. Indeed, research has shown that in one way or another, almost all of society's problems can be traced back to problems in the home.

All of this, however, is the "what" part of the story. There is so much more to the story that is left largely untold, so many big questions that have largely been unanswered. For starters, *when* did this destabilization start? Did it start fifty years ago? A hundred? A thousand? More?

Obviously, if God created marriage with Adam and Eve, then the attack on marriage must have come from Satan. But *why* is Satan attacking marriage? Who helped him? *Why* did they help him?

Furthermore, how did Satan manipulate mankind to the state we're at today, where all types of destabilizations of marriage are so commonplace, so normal, so *easily accepted?*

What is the story of Satan's battle against marriage, the Domestic Church?

Let's find out.

# I. In the Beginning

"In the beginning was the Word,
and the Word was with God,
and the Word was God."

John 1:1

BEFORE the creation of the heavens and the earth, there was God. Before there was light, there was God. Before there were angels and cherubim and seraphim, there was God. God who is eternal, He who has no beginning and no end, He who existed before all things.

God's desire was to love all He created, and be loved by all creation as the Creator. God knew that to be truly loved, He had to create beings with free will who would choose to love Him, because true love is a choice, not a command. In the depths of time, in the vast emptiness that always was, God's plan for everything came into being in an instant.

God knew that first He would create angels—pure spirits—of various ranks. He would give them all free will, and out of love for Him they would worship and serve Him and sing, "Holy, holy, holy is the Lord God almighty, who was, and who is, and who is to come! ... Worthy are you, Lord our God, to receive glory and honor and power, for you created all things; because of your will they came to be and were created."[5]

God knew that He would create one of the angels as the most perfect and beautiful of all the angels. He would be the dawn-bringer, Lucifer. God knew Lucifer would use his free will to look at himself and be filled with pride and vainglory. God knew Lucifer would see how the other angels worshipped God, and so Lucifer would begin to love himself so much that in his heart he would not be satisfied with his state of being. God knew Lucifer would want to be praised as God was, and worshipped as God was. God knew he would want to be like the Most High. God knew that Lucifer, the angel of light, would begin a rebellion against Him. God knew that he would begin to seduce other angels to join him, convincing them that they too could be like God. God knew that He would create another angel, Michael, who through his own free will would be the leader of those loyal to the Most High. God knew that when Michael had heard enough of the blasphemy, he would cry out a challenge to Lucifer: "Who is like God?"

God knew that out of his pride, Lucifer would reply, "I will not serve!" and the angels in legion with him would cry out, "We will not serve!" God knew that a great war would break out in Heaven between those who were faithful to Him, the Most High, and those who rebelled. God knew that in the end, Lucifer and the others in rebellion would be cast out of Heaven, and fall like lightning from the sky. God knew separation from Him would transform them from angels into demons, and He knew that He could use their rebellion to bring about a greater good.

God knew that after this battle, His next step would be to create the heavens and the earth, then light in the darkness, water and sky, and creatures in the sea and on the land and in the air. He knew then He would create man in His own image, give him a soul and free will and supernatural gifts, and place him in the middle of all creation. God knew that man would be alone, so He would create woman, and together they would fill His creation with souls designed to ascend to Heaven where they would love Him for all eternity. But God knew that the free will of all of these souls would need to be tested before they could join Him in Heaven. He knew that every soul would need to undergo the refiner's fire, that many souls would be lost because they would choose sin over Him, but those who endured would love Him perfectly for His goodness and His perfections. So He would give Lucifer—who would now be called Satan—access to His creation. Satan and his legion's purpose would be to test each soul for its true love of God.

God knew that the first perfect man would fall just like the perfect angel would fall, and his fall would cause all other generations of mankind to inherit a weakness toward rebellion. So God knew He would have to create a plan for salvation and redemption. He knew that this could only be accomplished by sending the perfect God-Man, the embodiment of both perfect spirit and perfect Man, who would be at the same time the perfect king and the perfect slave, who would be the model of both perfect leadership and perfect submission.

Since all souls would be created and tested, God knew that in order for these souls to return to Him, they would need to be taught of His goodness and perfections so that they might love Him. They must also be taught the story of rebellion against God, as well as the path to salvation. And each generation would need to pass on these teachings to those who came after them. God knew that He would need to establish a Church to perform this task. And the smallest form of His Church would be the family. These little Churches would have a name: marriages. They would be Domestic Churches. And they would be formed by the union of a husband and wife. Marriages would serve to teach children, by word and example, how to get to Heaven and how to form their own Domestic Church. The purpose of the Domestic Churches would be to raise saints, who would, in turn, raise future generations of saints.

God knew that these Domestic Churches would also be hated by Satan. They would be attacked continuously by the fallen angels until the very existence of the Domestic Church would come into question. God knew all of this in an instant. And because He is all good and all He does is good, He knew that in the end ... it would all be very good.

So God said, "Let there be."

And there was.

# II. The First Marriage

"Therefore a man
leaves his father and his mother
and cleaves to his wife,
and they become one flesh."[6]

Genesis 2:24

## II. The First Marriage

THE first act of Satan in the Bible was to attack Adam and Eve to cause their fall. Understanding and accepting the lessons and truths revealed in the story of creation and the fall of Adam and Eve is crucial to understanding how Satan attacks every marriage. In this chapter, we're going to look at Genesis 1, 2, and 3 and see what they have to teach us.

### THE CREATION OF ADAM & HIS MISSION

*"Then the Lord God formed the man out of the dust of the ground and blew into his nostrils the breath of life, and the man became a living being."[7] "The Lord God then took the man and settled him in the garden of Eden, to cultivate and care for it. The Lord God gave the man this order: You are free to eat from any of the trees of the garden except the tree of knowledge of good and evil. From that tree you shall not eat; when you eat from it you shall die. The Lord God said: It is not good for the man to be alone. I will make a helper suited to him. So the Lord God formed out of the ground all the wild animals and all the birds of the air, and he brought them to the man to see what he would call them; whatever the man called each living creature was then its name. The man gave names to all the tame animals, all the birds of the air, and all the wild animals."[8]*

Genesis 2 shows us the creation of Adam. We see God give him life when He breathed into Adam's nostrils. We see God give him his mission, to cultivate and care for the garden of Eden. We see God give Adam the bounds of his freedom with the commandment to not eat of the fruit of the tree of knowledge of good and evil. We also see God's intimate knowledge of Adam and his needs and God's grace in His desire to create a helper for Adam. Finally, we see Adam's authority since he was given the power to give names to all the animals, which were docile and under his command.

Formed in God's image, Adam was made perfect and infused with knowledge and intellect as the father of all mankind. Since he was created as an adult and had no one to learn from, Adam was gifted by God with a superior intellect and full knowledge of everything needed for the survival and propagation of the human race. This is referred to as the preternatural gift of infused knowledge. St. Thomas Aquinas argued that this knowledge was limited to those things necessary for his survival and the survival of the human race. He wasn't omnipotent as God is, so for example, he didn't know future events, couldn't know what was on the heart of another person, or how many hairs were on his own head. However, he would have known the difference between human hair and animal fur, and what properties different types of animal fur have and what different types of fur would be good for. He also would have known the nature of supernatural grace and how to preserve the sanctifying grace that is necessary to go to Heaven. This knowledge was Adam's to use and then pass on to his heirs for the good of all mankind.

At this point in creation history, Adam had no weaknesses. He was designed by God to live forever (Wisdom 2:23). There was no sickness, no injury, no pain, and work was not a fatigue but a joy. "The Council of Trent declared that man was constituted in holiness and justice. This justice and holiness were not a necessary part of his nature, but were freely bestowed upon him by God."[9] The justice and holiness that Adam was given would have made him in total control of his emotions and rational thought. He wouldn't have been able to be deceived, or confused, or allow his imagination to influence his actions. The supernatural grace of being perfectly ordered, along with his superior intellect and faultless reason, made Adam immune to temptation by trickery or deceit. His will was fully under his control, free from all weakness, and it was not disordered by sensual desires. And, like the angels before him, Adam possessed the free will to choose to know, love, and serve God.

He was, however, the only one of his race. Even though Adam was surrounded by all of the creatures of creation, who were all also living in perfect harmony, he was still alone.

### THE CREATION OF EVE

*"But none proved to be a helper suited to the man. So the Lord God cast a deep sleep on the man, and while he was asleep, he took out one of his ribs and closed up its place with flesh. The Lord God then built the rib that he had taken from the man into a woman. When he brought her to the man, the man said: 'This one, at last, is bone of my bones, and flesh of my flesh; This one shall be called "woman," for out of man this one has been taken.' That is why a man leaves his father and mother and clings to his wife, and the two of them become one body."* [10]

Here we see the perfection of God's plan. God, being infinitely perfect always knew that Adam would need a helper, and He also knew that none of the animals would be a suitable helper. So this raises some questions:

1. Why did He wait to create Eve? Why bring all the animals to Adam first?

   In showing Adam all of the creatures, He was preparing Adam for the creation of Eve. God was showing Adam that nothing else would be suitable for him, so that when Eve was created, Adam would rejoice in her. At the same time Adam would be fortified in his knowledge of God's greatness and love for him.

2. Why take Adam's rib to form Eve?

   Clearly, God could have just made Eve from the dust of the ground as He had Adam. God has a purpose and meaning in everything He does, and so He chose to use Adam's rib for a specific reason. A study of human anatomy classifies bones into three categories based on purpose: bones that support weight, bones that assist in movement, and bones that protect. If God had taken a bone that supported weight or assisted in movement, it would have left Adam crippled in a physical way. Only the skull and ribs are classified as bones that protect, and let us note that God chose a rib bone, which protects the heart. Throughout the Bible, the heart is spoken of as the will of a person, and a clear distinction made over and over again between heart and mind. If we believe that the heart is the center of our emotions, then in using man's rib bone to create woman God created them so that not only do they become one flesh (Ephesians 5:31), they are bound at the heart, bound by love. This unity comes at a price: for the two to become one, Adam's heart is now exposed. By God's design, the person who both protected Adam's heart, and the person who was most easily able to access it, was Eve.

3. Was Eve the same as Adam?

Like Adam, Eve was designed for immortality. She was also created free from sickness, injury, pain, and fatigue. Eve also had the graces of being perfectly ordered, of superior intellect, and possessing faultless reason.

**GOD'S BLESSING AND COMMAND**

*"God blessed them and God said to them: Be fertile and multiply; fill the earth and subdue it. Have dominion over the fish of the sea, the birds of the air, and all the living things that crawl on the earth."* [11]

God's first blessing upon mankind was upon man and woman as husband and wife. This blessing made them fertile, and it was the same blessing and command that he gave to the fish and the birds. But mankind was also given the authority to subdue the earth and have dominion over it, as earth was created by God's goodness for the sake of man.

This blessing, and all the gifts God gave Adam and Eve, were not meant to be theirs alone. They were designed by God to be passed down to their heirs. All the children of Adam and Eve were destined to be blessed with fruitfulness and authority over the earth. All their descendants were to inherit perfect justice, reason, and freedom from sickness, injury, pain, and death. The supernatural gifts given to Adam and Eve and due their descendants had one condition: obedience.

### ORIGINAL SIN

*"Now the snake was the most cunning of all the wild animals that the Lord God had made. He asked the woman, 'Did God really say, "You shall not eat from any of the trees in the garden"?' The woman answered the snake: 'We may eat of the fruit of the trees in the garden; it is only about the fruit of the tree in the middle of the garden that God said, "You shall not eat it or even touch it, or else you will die."' But the snake said to the woman: 'You certainly will not die! God knows well that when you eat of it your eyes will be opened and you will be like gods, who know good and evil.' The woman saw that the tree was good for food and pleasing to the eyes, and the tree was desirable for gaining wisdom. So she took some of its fruit and ate it; and she also gave some to her husband, who was with her, and he ate it. Then the eyes of both of them were opened, and they knew that they were naked; so they sewed fig leaves together and made loincloths for themselves.*

*"When they heard the sound of the Lord God walking about in the garden at the breezy time of the day, the man and his wife hid themselves from the Lord God among the trees of the garden. The Lord God then called to the man and asked him: Where are you? He answered, 'I heard you in the garden; but I was afraid, because I was naked, so I hid.' Then God asked: Who told you that you were naked? Have you eaten from the tree of which I had forbidden you to eat? The man replied, 'The woman whom you put here with me—she gave me fruit from the tree, so I ate it.' The Lord God then asked the woman: What is this you have done? The woman answered, 'The snake tricked me, so I ate it.'"* [12]

Mankind was destined from his creation for Heaven. "But by the envy of the devil, death entered the world."[13] Satan wanted to prevent Adam and Eve—and all of their descendants—from attaining the beatific vision. He wanted to prevent all of us from attaining the unity with God which he had lost forever in his fall from Heaven. This is Satan's mission: to divide us from God. And as we will see, he does this by attacking the family, the Domestic Church.

Satan shows us here his three tactics for causing people to sin:

1.  He creates doubt about truth

    "Did God really say, 'You shall not eat from any of the trees in the garden'?" Eve never heard God's command. Adam did. It was Adam's responsibility to properly instruct Eve and ensure she understood God's command. Satan used this gap in her knowledge to cast doubt on what Eve had been taught to be truth.

2.  He creates fear about everything good.

    "God knows well that when you eat of it your eyes will be opened and you will be like gods, who know good and evil." The tree was no doubt beautiful. The state of all of creation and the order of it was perfect and beautiful, beyond anything we can ever imagine. God created it; therefore it had to be beautiful. And Eve's state in life was not just good, but "very good" (Genesis 1:31). But Satan created the fear in Eve that God was holding back and that she was missing out on something bigger, something better. Satan was, in effect, calling God a liar.

3.  He takes everything beautiful and distorts and disfigures it with lies.

    "You certainly will not die!" The beautiful perfection of Eden rested in its perfect order, where the will was subordinated to perfect reason and where all of creation, from God down to the smallest pebble, was aligned in the hierarchy as God had designed.

Internally, God designed Adam and Eve so that their will was subject to their perfectly formed reason. This internal hierarchy was designed to allow all of mankind to make perfect, sinless choices in our lives. By appealing to Eve's emotions and persuading her to accept the lie, Satan disfigured this perfect hierarchy and caused Eve (and then Adam) to question their right reason. He distorted their right reason with emotion, and as a result, their will became subject to their emotion instead of their reason.

Notice that Satan did not call into question the existence of God. This, Adam and Eve could have easily rejected by their own senses. Neither did Satan call into question the authority of God, because this Adam and Eve could have rejected by their supernatural intellect and reason. Instead, Satan used the only thing available to him. Because Adam and Eve were not omnipotent as God is, they lacked the ability to understand what lies in the heart of another. Satan exploited this to cause Adam and Eve to question God's goodness and trustworthiness; he was able to attack their perception of God. Their perception about truth, their perception about what God created as good, and their perception about what was beautiful were all distorted by Satan.

How was Satan able to accomplish this? How was he able to distort their perception? Let us remember that because God is all good and can only do good, He did not create evil; evil is simply the absence of good. Adam and Eve were surrounded with only that which was perfect, true, good, and beautiful. They had no concept of death because everything around them was alive. They had no concept of evil because everything around them was good. So when Satan approached Eve, she had no reason to believe that he was dangerous. Her perfectly formed logic would have reassured her that God has created everything; everything God created is true, good, and beautiful; and because God must have created this other being it too must be true, good, and beautiful. She would have no reason to suspect that this other being was not telling her the truth, because it was created good. She would have trusted her husband was also telling her the truth, that God told him that even if the fruit of the tree was touched, then they would die. Her perception was that God said that touching the fruit would lead to death and her perception was that Satan was telling the truth.

Her faulty perception led to the five sins of Eve as acknowledged by St. Ambrose, St. Ignatius of Antioch, St. John Chrysostom, and St. Augustine: 1) Pride because she looked at her own excellence and desired equality with God; 2) Impatience because she was prohibited access to something that was so good; 3) Curiosity because she wanted knowledge outside of her state in life; 4) Gluttony because while God gave Adam and Eve everything in abundance, she desired more; and 5) Error in understanding because God's command was that you shall not *eat* of the fruit, but Eve said that "God said, 'You shall not eat it *or even touch it,* or else you will die.'" (Emphasis added.) According to St. Thomas Aquinas, there was also a sixth sin: 6) Intentional scandal because "the woman not only herself sinned, but suggested sin to the man; wherefore she sinned against both God and her neighbor."[14] (As St. Thomas teaches, scandal referred to here is defined as occurring whenever "a man either intends, by his evil word or deed, to lead another man into sin, or, if he does not so intend, when his deed is of such a nature as to lead another into sin."[15])

Let us examine Eve's fifth sin, error in understanding. The commandment was given to Adam. It was *his* responsibility to instruct Eve and ensure she understood it properly. Scripture is not clear if Adam instructed her properly, and Eve did not understand it, or if out of love for her and desire for her protection, Adam embellished God's commandment. Before she ate the fruit, she had to touch it. So when she *touched* the fruit and did not die—which Adam told her was God's command—it gave her further reason to believe Satan's lie that eating the fruit would make her like a god, and that she would not die. Whether she improperly understood Adam or he embellished God's command, either way, it was *Adam's* failure to ensure that Eve knew the commandment of God, *as instructed by God.* Before Adam ate the fruit, he was already complicit in the sin of Eve because God gave Adam responsibility for Eve.

Whereas Eve had six sins, the saints tell us that Adam had eight sins. Like, Eve, Adam was guilty of 1) Pride 2) Curiosity and 3) Gluttony. Adam also had sins of 4) Unbelief, that what God told him wasn't the whole truth; 5) Presumption, that God would forgive him for disobedience; 6) Disobedience; 7) Making excuses and blaming Eve for his sin; and 8) Excessive desire to please his wife. Adam was also guilty of 9) Unintentional scandal, because his failure to ensure Eve properly understood God's command led her to sin.

Let's look at Adam's eighth sin. It is not a sin for someone to want to please his spouse, and when something is done as an act of charity, it is a very good thing. However, when an act is done out of such excessive desire that the desire to please leads to a sinful act, the excessive desire becomes a sin in and of itself. In Adam's case, he prioritized the desire to please Eve by eating the fruit over the desire to obey God by keeping His commandment. In putting Eve ahead of God and disobeying what he knew to be God's law, Adam turned Eve into an idol. He perceived that none of what he was doing was truly a sin that would result in death.

Make no mistake that Adam and Eve did not casually eat of the fruit. It was a deliberate, thoughtful act of contemplation. Remember that they were *both* given the supernatural grace of perfect reason and control of their wills. The wording of Scripture suggests that Eve was not by the tree when she was tempted; she referred to the tree as "the tree in the middle of the garden" instead of "that tree" or "this tree." Adam never conversed with Satan in Scripture, so we cannot tell if

Adam was with her or not when she was tempted, only that he was with her when she ate. Regardless, time had to elapse between the temptation of Eve and her decision to ignore her perfectly ordered reason, walk over to the tree, and eat of the fruit. Also, since Satan never spoke to Adam, effort must have been made on Eve's part to persuade Adam to ignore his perfectly ordered reason. "The wills of our first parents were not weakened by any disordered sensual desires. Adam and Eve could not commit sin lightly; to commit a sin cost them as much effort as it costs us to perform a good deed."[16] "Behind the disobedient choice of our first parents lurks a seductive voice, opposed to God, which makes them fall into death out of envy."[17]

Even before God's justice, when they ate of the tree, Adam and Eve immediately lost *all* the supernatural gifts God gave them: "Then the eyes of both of them were opened." These gifts are called supernatural because they are not part of their created nature; instead, they are powers that elevated them above their created state. When they chose to disobey God, Adam and Eve did permanent damage to their souls, resulting in the loss of these supernatural gifts:

1. They lost the light of understanding, and with it the ability to clearly understand God, the truths about Him such as his love for mankind and infinite goodness, the purpose for creation, and more.

2. Their wills lost harmony with and order under rational reason, leaving them weak and able to be swayed by their imaginations.

3. Their weakened intellect and will became prone to temptation by Satan.

4. They lost supernatural grace, becoming displeasing to God and barred forever from Heaven.

Now that their eyes were opened and they lost these supernatural gifts, Adam and Eve suddenly felt shame in their nakedness. "Because man rebelled against God, in punishment his own flesh rose in rebellion against his reason, and so man became ashamed of his own flesh."[18] Because of Original Sin, we are no longer born children of God but instead children of wrath (Ephesians 2:3).

Because Satan chose to attack Adam and Eve's *perception* of God, their perception of *everything* became distorted. In allowing their perception of God—who is all-perfect and all-good—to become distorted, from that point forward *all* of their perceptions would become distorted, including their perception of good and evil. These weaknesses were then passed along to all of us. Thanks to Adam and Eve, our perception, understanding, and acceptance of God's truth is now dark and clouded. Our wills are now swayed by imagination and emotion. We are now easily confused by the lies and tricks of Satan. Our bodies now suffer sickness, injury, pain, and death. We are all indeed the poor banished children of Eve, and as heirs of Adam and Eve, with the exception of Jesus Christ and the Blessed Mother, we are all are now conceived in a state of Original Sin, lacking God's sanctifying grace, and we inherit the same punishment as was given to our original parents.

### GOD'S JUSTICE

Because God is infinitely just, He not only had to punish Adam and Eve's disobedience, but administer a punishment that would fit their crime.

*"To the woman he said:*

> *I will intensify your toil in childbearing;*
> *in pain you shall bring forth children.*
> *Yet your urge shall be for your husband,*
> *and he shall rule over you."*[19]

As a woman, Eve's role in creation was to bring new human lives to the world, and not just any lives but lives designed for immortal life in Heaven. Instead, her disobedience brought the pains of death. So in the first part of God's punishment for Eve, He made her—and all women who followed her except the Blessed Mother—endure the pains of childbirth. In the second part of God's punishment for Eve, because she was unsatisfied with her state in life, because she desired to rise up and be "as a god," God ensured that while she would continue to have the desire to rule over Adam, he would still rule over her.

*"To the man he said: Because you listened to your wife and ate from the tree about which I commanded you, 'You shall not eat from it,'*

> *Cursed is the ground because of you!*
> *In toil you shall eat its yield all the days of your life.*
>
> *Thorns and thistles it shall bear for you,*
> *and you shall eat the grass of the field.*
>
> *By the sweat of your brow you shall eat bread,*
> *Until you return to the ground, from which you were taken;*
> *For you are dust, and to dust you shall return."* [20]

Like God's punishment for Eve, Adam's punishment fit his crime. So long as he kept God's one commandment, Adam never had to toil for the abundance of food God provided him in Eden, never had to endure fatigue, never had to experience pain. This just punishment means Adam must struggle for his food through difficult, painful work. Also, in His infinite justice, God kept His word: Adam would endure not just a spiritual death but a physical one. Since Eve involved Adam in her sin and they were united as one flesh, Adam's punishment also applied to Eve and as our original parents their punishments and Original Sin are inherited by us.

What must be further noted is how God began His punishment for Adam: "Because you listened to your wife..." Even if Eve was confused, *Adam knew clearly, without question, what God's commandment was regarding the fruit of the tree.* What is the significance of this part of the punishment, then? First, Adam listened to Eve instead of God. Second, Adam had been given his authority to lead by God, but with that authority came the responsibility of taking care of whom God gave him. Adam neither obeyed God nor took charge and care. Rather than lead his wife away from sin, he chose to allow Eve to do something *he knew* violated the command of God and even allowed her to persuade him to do the same. What's more, after committing this sin, Adam tried to shift the blame to Eve rather than have the integrity to own up to his own error: "The woman whom you put here with me—she gave me fruit from the tree."[21]

Adam gave up his authority, then tried to escape his responsibility. Ultimately, this is why Adam gets the full blame for Original Sin. Monsignor Charles Pope writes, "It is clearly a sin that involved both of them. And yet, both in Scripture and Tradition when this sin is referred to formally by name it is called the 'Sin of Adam' or 'Adam's Sin.' It is also described as coming to us 'through one man' not 'through Adam and Eve' or 'through a man and a woman.' ... Now, to be sure, both Scripture and the Catechism describe the Sin as involving both Adam and Eve, but neither formally refer to it as the 'Sin of Adam and Eve' but only, the 'Sin of Adam' or 'Adam's Sin.' Sin comes to us through Adam."[22]

## THE LASTING EFFECTS OF ORIGINAL SIN

Even if only one of our original parents had eaten, but the other did not, there still would have been at the very least a strain upon their marriage, would there not? Wouldn't the one who stayed true have been ever distrustful of the one who sinned, even though they had only sinned once? What we do know is that Satan's first attack on marriage was successful. Even if only one had sinned, Satan still would have succeeded in damaging their marriage by dividing husband and wife against each other, and in so doing, dividing them both from God.

All that God had given to Adam was destined for Adam's children and heirs. All the graces, all the perfections, were ours to inherit. But with the loss of those graces through Original Sin, and with it God's just punishment of Adam and Eve, we inherit their punishment: every child would be conceived with Original Sin.

But for the sake of our salvation, there would be an exception. Actually, two.

# III. God's Plan for Salvation

"See what love the Father has bestowed on us
that we may be called the children of God."

I John 3:1

# III. God's Plan for Salvation

THE greatness of a parent's love for his children can only be compared with the vastness of the oceans. Only the love for God should be greater than a parent's love for his children. How vast, then, is God's love for each and every one of us? The Bible is God's love story, telling us how much He loves us. And every part of the Bible—indeed, every story, every character, every sentence, and every word—is the inspired and inerrant word of God. Nothing is in the Bible that is unimportant. Neither is there anything missing. The entirety of the Old Testament points in one direction, to one thing and one thing only: Jesus Christ, whose birth, death, and resurrection made it possible for all of us to reach the beatific vision in Heaven. It is essential to understand the Old Testament in order to fully appreciate Christ and the New Covenant. Delving deeply into the Old Testament has been the work of countless theologians and scholars. While we don't have the time and space to fully explore the Old Testament here, we'll focus on a few points to demonstrate how God's plan for salvation came to be and how this relates to marriage.

## THE WAGES OF SIN ARE DEATH

From the beginning, God had planned for our salvation, and the Old Testament chronicles the progression of that plan. From Adam and Eve through the Age of the Patriarchs, God spoke directly with the heads of families to give them His law. The Patriarch would then pass on God's law to his family. This was the earliest form of catechesis, and it could also be considered the first form of the Domestic Church. The righteous followed God's laws and were blessed, while the wicked ignored God's laws and were destroyed. Once someone lost friendship with God due to sin, there was no way to get it back. These souls would be destined for the Hell of the Damned.

The story of the Israelites' captivity in Egypt and journey from the Passover to the Promised Land began to give us glimpses of God's plan for our salvation: the sacrifice of the Passover lamb, the perpetual celebration of unleavened bread, the manna, the Ark of the Covenant, the tabernacle, the life-giving water in the desert, and many others. It also was the first time that God's laws were written down; Moses is believed to have written the first five books of the Bible (known as the Pentateuch) which recorded the oral history, law, and tradition of the Patriarchs. The Exodus also marked a turning point in God's plan, where for the first time mankind would be able to atone for sin by a blood sacrifice. By bringing different sacrificial offerings to the Levite priests, they could return to a state of friendship with God, though Original Sin remained on their souls.

From the Age of the Patriarchs, through the Age of the Prophets, to the end of the Old Testament, everyone who was in God's favor and judged at their death to be in friendship with God still had some degree of sin on their souls, even if only Original Sin. From the beginning to the end of the Old Testament, all of these souls went to the Limbo of the Fathers, which is considered to be the upper edge of Hell. These souls were perfectly happy and not suffering any of the pains of the Hell of the Damned, but they were still separated from the beatific vision, prevented from being in communion with God in Heaven while they awaited their redemption.

### THE NEW ADAM

To complete His plan for salvation, God always intended to send a savior to redeem us. Because of God's infinite justice, the only acceptable savior would be the Second Person of the Holy Trinity, God the Son, who would fulfill all promises and prophecies. The New Covenant of Jesus Christ would open the doors to Heaven that the sin of Adam had closed. Jesus Christ, the incarnation of the ever-living God, would come as the New Adam to save us from sin and death. But even in this human form, His holiness would still be infinite and everlasting. It would have to be.

The Old Testament has provided theologians numerous examples of the prefigurement of Jesus Christ in human form. But it also has provided us numerous examples of God's immeasurable holiness. Indeed, God is infinitely holy. From the idol of Dagon being broken to pieces in front of the Ark of the Covenant in I Samuel 5, to Uzzah being struck dead from simply touching the Ark in II Samuel 6, it is clear that God's holiness is literally a life-and-death matter. It is so serious, in fact, that Levite priests performing their work in the veiled area of the temple called "the Holy of Holies" would be struck dead by God if they did something improperly. So they wore bells on their vestments and a rope around their ankle while behind the curtain. If the bells stopped ringing, the people on the other side of the curtain knew that the priest did something wrong and was killed. And the rope? It was so the dead body could be dragged out and another Levite priest would go in to take his place. Obviously, God takes His holiness seriously.

God was, is, and always will remain infinitely holy. He cannot sin nor be tempted to sin. He cannot deceive nor be deceived. He cannot defile nor be defiled. God loves His own perfections infinitely; if this were not true, if there were anything about Himself that He did not love, then God would cease to be perfect. So when the time came for God to send the Second Person of the Holy Trinity to dwell among us as one of us, it only stands to reason that He would be sure to surround Himself with holiness.

## A RIGHTEOUS MAN
God the Father needed someone to serve as the father of the Messiah. From Sacred Scripture, we know that he had to be from the royal house of David in order to fulfill prophecy. But was this alone good enough to be the head of the Holy Family? Was his family lineage enough to make him fit to model God the Father for the child Jesus? Sacred Scripture says no. In St. Matthew's Gospel, St. Joseph is referred to as "a righteous man" (Matthew 1:19). In all his actions, St. Joseph proved his

righteousness by humbly following the commands and commandments of God without error. After all, this was the man whom the child Jesus was to honor on earth by obeying his every command. In order for Jesus to be perfect, He would have to perfectly follow all the commandments *and* perfectly obey his father St. Joseph, prior to submitting to the will of God the Father during His public ministry. If St. Joseph were to tell or allow the child Jesus to do something sinful, even in the slightest, that would create an impossible paradox: Jesus, the Second Person of the Holy Trinity, God incarnate, could neither sin by disobeying his father St. Joseph, nor sin by committing an act that was sinful in and of itself, thus violating the law of God the Father. So the Church fathers have long held that St. Joseph was blessed by God with the graces necessary to lead a life completely free of sin. This is why St. Matthew refers to St. Joseph as "a righteous man." As the father of the child Jesus, there could be no one less.

### A WOMAN FULL OF GRACE

"And the angel being come in, said unto her: Hail, full of grace, the Lord is with thee: blessed art thou among women."[23] This is the greeting the angel Gabriel gave to Mary, and it continues to show the infinite holiness of God. For the woman destined to be the mother of God, no one of lesser existence would be good enough. To begin with, she would need to be given the graces to lead a life completely free from sin, just like St. Joseph and for the same reason. But a careful study of the inspired, inerrant Word of God shows that Mary was especially favored by God, because she *had* to be. The first thing to note is that where St. Joseph is referred to as "righteous", Mary is referred to as "full of grace." Not just possessing grace, but *full* of grace. As St. Thomas Aquinas observed, in the Old Testament men revered angels, but the angel Gabriel's greeting of Mary showed that he was revering *her*. In a study of the original Greek, the Greek word for "endowed with grace" is used in what is called the "perfect tense", meaning it was both a completed and continuing action, not one that had happened, is happening, or will happen. This means that Mary was always and continued to be "completely, perfectly, enduringly endowed with grace."[24] Recalling what we know about God's holiness reveals why this must be.

First, looking back to the Old Testament, even the Kohathites could not touch the sacred objects or they would die. Uzzah died from simply touching the Ark of the Covenant. This was because, due to Original Sin we are "children of wrath," who are born enemies of God. If such harsh punishment was due for those who touch holy *objects*, what must be the punishment for coming into contact with holiness itself? Mary would be carrying *God*—holiness incarnate—in her womb. Since Original Sin makes us children of wrath and enemies of God, could a woman who was a child of wrath and enemy of God carry the Second Person of the Trinity in her womb for even a second and not die out of God's perfect and infinite justice?

Second, because God is infinitely holy, He can neither defile nor be defiled. In the book of Job we read, "Who can bring a clean thing out of an unclean? There is not one." (Job 14:4 RSVCE) Jesus is fully man and fully God. Jesus' humanity was derived from Mary, His mother. If she were defiled by Original Sin, how then could Jesus be made clean when He was conceived in she who was unclean? We see later in Scripture that the body of our Lord was laid in a tomb that was undefiled because even His dead body was holy and must not be defiled. If His *dead* body could not be defiled because it was holy, how, then could holiness incarnate spend nine months in the womb of a woman who was born an enemy of God, defiled by sin?

Third, let us take a look at the Ark of the Covenant in the Old Testament with a brief study of Scripture. The Ark was God's presence in humanity's midst, the dwelling place of God among the Israelites. Construction of the Ark was finished in Exodus 37, and it was placed in the Tabernacle in Exodus 40. The Ark contained the word of God in stone (the Ten Commandments), a jar of manna, and Aaron's rod that blossomed. In the New Testament, the word of God was embodied in Jesus, who is the fulfillment of the law (Matthew 5:17). Jesus is also the new manna, the new life-giving bread from Heaven (John 6:31-35). Aaron's rod was a staff showing the authority of the high priest. That Aaron's rod was dead and then sprung to life also prefigured Jesus Christ, the most authoritative high priest (Hebrews 4:14) who died and then rose to life.

Using a type of scriptural study known as "typology"—recognizing where the New Testament is concealed in the Old Testament, and the Old Testament is revealed in the New Testament—we see that the Ark of the Covenant is an Old Testament foreshadowing of Mary, who was the Ark of the New Covenant, carrying the fulfillment of the law, the new manna, and the most authoritative high priest in her womb. There are many Scriptural references that show this connection; let us examine just three:

1.  II Samuel 6:2-6 & Luke 1:41

    In the Old Testament, the Ark of the Covenant had been lost for three months. When King David found the Ark, it was being moved on a cart pulled by oxen instead of being moved by men, as God instructed. The Israelites were celebrating the finding of the Ark, which caused the oxen to start to kick and tip the cart. The Greek word used to describe the oxen kicking was the same Greek word used to describe John the Baptist kicking inside Elizabeth's womb at Mary's arrival. In essence, the arrival of Jesus caused John the Baptist to "kick like an ox."

2.  II Samuel 6:9 & Luke 1:43

    Compare King David's words of excitement upon finding the Ark: "How can the ark of the Lord come to me?"[25] with Elizabeth's word, upon the arrival of Mary: "And how does this happen to me, that the mother of my Lord should come to me?"[26] It should also be noted that the town where David found the Ark was the same town where Zechariah and Elizabeth lived.

3.  Exodus 40:34 & Luke 1:35 & John 1:14

    When Moses completed the tent of meeting, "the cloud covered the tent of meeting, and the glory of the Lord filled the tabernacle."[27] When the angel Gabriel was speaking to Mary, he told her that "The holy Spirit will come upon you, and the power of the Most High will overshadow you."[28] John tells us in his Gospel that "the Word became flesh and made his dwelling among us."[29] The literal translation of "made his dwelling" is to "pitch his tent/tabernacle."[30]

Mary, as the Ark of the New Covenant, carried the Lord Jesus within her womb. Adam and Eve had brought sin and death to all mankind through their disobedience. Jesus, the perfect Son, brought salvation for all mankind by His obedience to God and His perfect fulfillment of prophecy. And Mary, the perfect daughter of God the Father, perfect spouse of the Holy Spirit, and perfect Mother of God the Son, brought eternal life into the world by her obedience to God and acceptance of His will. "Behold the handmaid of the Lord: be it done to me according to thy word."[31]

## A HOLY FAMILY

When Jesus came to us, it created a situation that was quite phenomenal. Speaking on the Gospel of Luke, St. Cyril of Alexandria in the 5th Century said:

*"Look closely how profound this dispensation is: the Word tolerates being born in human fashion, although in his divine nature he has no beginning and is not subject to time. He who as God is all perfect, submits to bodily growth: the Incorporeal has limbs that advance to the ripeness of manhood. He is filled*

*with wisdom who is himself all wisdom. What can we say to this? By these things he who was in the form of the Father is made like us. The Rich is in poverty; the High is in humiliation."* [32]

Throughout their life together, it is clear that Jesus, Mary, and Joseph were a holy family. They obeyed everything proscribed by Jewish law and tradition. Joseph showed by his silent example his obedience to God and his acceptance of his responsibility to be a righteous steward of his family. Mary showed us by her example her obedience to God and submission to the leadership of her husband Joseph, even though she was blessed with far more holiness and grace than he was. And Jesus showed us by His example what it means to be an obedient son, even though He was the greatest member of the family.

### I Am the Living Bread

Christ's obedience to God the Father by His Baptism in the Jordan showed us the way to cleanse our souls from Original Sin and to receive from God an infusion of sanctifying grace and the virtues necessary to get to Heaven. This sacrament would keep us out of Limbo, and indeed is necessary for salvation. But Baptism alone is not enough to get us into Heaven. As Christ said in Matthew 5:17, "Do not think that I have come to abolish the law or the prophets. I have come not to abolish but to fulfill." Therefore, everything that God told the Patriarchs in the oral law was and still is in force; God's everlasting covenant with Abraham was and still is everlasting; and everything God proscribed to Moses to be observed throughout the generations as a statute forever would still need to be observed forever.

Jesus Christ came as the new Adam, the wholly obedient first-born Son. He came to be the new manna, the new bread from Heaven. Indeed, in Bethlehem (which means "house of bread"), our Savior—who was born our bread of life—was laid in a manger from which cattle ate. The symbology is unmistakable. He came to be the living water that gives us eternal life in the desert of sin. He came to join the oral law and tradition of the Patriarchs to the written law and tradition of the Israelites, to unite the royal priesthood of Melchizedek with the Levitical priesthood, to fuse bread with flesh and wine with blood. Yes, Christ is the bread of Melchizedek and the flesh of Passover lamb, the wine of Melchizedek and the blood of the lamb. His death on Calvary shed enough blood to cover all the sins of all mankind, once and for everyone, so that we might all be free from the bondage of sin and the pains of eternal death.

## CHRIST RAISES THE STAKES

So it was after Christ's physical death that Satan had a major problem. Satan's main goal is to prevent *any* soul from attaining the beatific vision, and as we know, souls in Limbo were not capable of attaining the beatific vision. For Satan, souls with Original Sin and trapped in Limbo were almost as good as souls in the Hell of the Damned. Christ changed all this. In the Apostles Creed, "[w]hen we say that Christ descended into Hell we mean that, after He died, the soul of Christ descended into a place or state of rest, called Limbo, where the souls of the just were waiting for Him. Heaven had been closed by the sin of Adam. The just among the dead could not enter Heaven until Christ satisfied for man's sin and repaired its injuries. They awaited their redemption in Limbo."[33] After His physical death but prior to His resurrection, Christ descended to the Limbo of the Fathers and emptied it of all the just souls trapped there. They were now partakers in the beatific vision. For Satan, that was infuriating. But for him, it was about to get much, much worse.

By His participation in Baptism, Jesus made it a Sacramental part of God's plan of salvation. By His presence and the performance of His first miracle at the wedding at Cana, Jesus also made marriage a Sacramental part of God's plan of salvation. And at the Last Supper, the Eucharist, which Christ instituted among us, became not only our daily bread and our sacrificial wine, but also our atonement for sins. But Christ went further with the Eucharist than with the other Sacraments: by telling us that "unless you eat the flesh of the Son of Man and drink his blood, you do not have life within you."[34] He elevated the Eucharist beyond just a Sacramental *part* of God's plan for our salvation; He made it *essential* to our salvation.

After His resurrection, through the Apostles and Apostolic succession, Christ established His everlasting Church to bring these and other essential Sacraments to the whole world. His Church and the works of the Apostles and their descendants would now allow the souls who had maintained friendship with God to attain the beatific vision so long as they died in a state of sanctifying grace; after death, they would no longer be stuck in Limbo. That was a situation Satan could not sit idly by and allow to happen. With Christ and the New Covenant, the stakes were raised. For Satan, the war had now escalated, and he was not about to back down.

Satan tried to stop the spread of Christianity. He used non-Christian ideologies and false religions to persecute the original Christians and the early Church. These included first the Jews and Romans, then, as the centuries went on, the Persians, Muslims, and various pagan nations. As time went by and Christ's Church grew, Satan realized that he couldn't stop the spread of Christianity by force. No. He realized that he would have to go back to the playbook where he first found success. He would need to attack our perceptions of good and evil and our perception of God. And he would do this by attacking husband and wife.

# IV. Weakened Walls

"Where there is division and anger,
God does not dwell."

St. Ignatius of Antioch

SINCE the Levite priests in the days of Moses, God established a singular, visible faith. Jesus Christ, the Messiah, came and fulfilled prophecy, for the first time extending that faith outward beyond the Jews and bringing the possibility of salvation to all. Before he was betrayed, He prayed to God the Father: "I pray not only for them, but also for those who will believe in me through their word, so that they may all be one, as you, Father, are in me and I in you, that they also may be in us, that the world may believe that you sent me. And I have given them the glory you gave me, so that they may be one, as we are one, I in them and you in me, that they may be brought to perfection as one, that the world may know that you sent me, and that you loved them even as you loved me." [35]

Reverend Spirago comments:

*"The Church is the body of Christ. This fact is asserted frequently in Sacred Scripture: 'He is the head of his body, the Church' (Colossians 1:18); 'For as the body is one and has many members, and all the members of the body, many as they are, form one body, so also it is with Christ' (I Corinthians 12:12). The mystical body, the Church, is like a human body. Many members and organs form a human body, yet they are quickened by the same spirit; the faithful are individually the members of Christ and together make one body of Christ, because they are all imbued with the Holy Spirit. And this body is visible. The Church is visible precisely because she is a body. The Fathers of the Church speak in the same strain. St. Augustine declares that the whole Christ is both head and body: the head, that Savior who has ascended into Heaven; the body, the Church which labors here on earth. Between the head and the body there can be no interstice. Christ is the foundation; we are the superstructure. He is the vine, we are the branches.... This union is so close that Christ and the society which is His body form one mystical being. Christ Himself likens it to the oneness of the Father with the Son." [36]*

The establishment of the New Covenant made it possible for souls to get to Heaven with the help of men in the form of consecrated religious who serve Christ's Church. God now had the help of more than just the Levite priests, but as the Church grew, there was an ever-growing number of people to help God save souls.

### SATAN'S DILEMMA

Satan's objective is simple: division. He wants to divide the body from the head. He wants to divide us from God. He wants to divide us from truth. He wants to divide us from Christ's Church. Where Jesus brought mankind unity with Him through the establishment of the Eucharist—so that He may be always with us and in us—Satan wants to divide us from the very thing that united the early Church and strengthened it against brutal persecutions. Satan cannot win by attacking the institutional Church since Christ Himself is protecting it and strengthens us in the Eucharist. So Satan has set out to destroy the Domestic Church. He wants to divide husband from wife and parent from child. He knows the destruction of the Domestic Church will divide us from Christ's Church, keeping us from the Eucharist, keeping us from the Sacraments, and ultimately, keeping us from Heaven.

Satan realized that if he was going to succeed in destroying souls, he also would need the help of people to destroy the souls of *other* people. God has helpers, so Satan decided to get some of his own. He knew that if he could win enough influential voices, and if those voices spoke from minds of distorted thought, and if they were motivated by hearts corrupted by pride, *his* sin, then he could subtly drag millions of families and billions of souls to the Hell of the Damned.

St. John Paul II said:

*"This battle against the devil which characterizes the Archangel Michael is still going on, because the devil is still alive and at work in [the] world. In fact, the evil that is in it, the disorder we see in society, the infidelity of man, the*

*interior fragmentation of which he is a victim, are not merely the consequences of Original Sin, but also the effect of the dark and infesting activity of Satan, of this saboteur of man's moral equilibrium. St. Paul does not hesitate to call him 'the god of this world' (II Corinthians 4:4), inasmuch as he shows himself to be an astute enchanter, capable of insinuating himself into our actions so as to introduce deviations that are as destructive as they are apparently conformed to our instinctive aspirations."* [37]

Satan's plan is one of stealth. He knew that a direct confrontation wouldn't work, at least not initially. If people realized they were being attacked, they'd put their defenses up quickly. No, Satan knew he had to be patient. He knew that he had to work slowly, under the radar, so as not to draw our attention. There are just too many people in Christ's Church to hold it up from his attacks. He knew that the only way to defeat Christ's Church would be to empty it. And to empty the Church, he needed to be so subtle that no one would put up a fight. He needed to be so clever that no one would even be aware we were being attacked. To empty the Church, he would need to destroy the family, the Domestic Church, which forms the basis of Christ's Church. And he would need to take his time.

## SATAN DIVIDES

When God created Adam and Eve, He made them perfect. Their marriage was the first Domestic Church, the smallest body of the faithful. God built this first Domestic Church of rock. Their supernatural knowledge of truth was the flawless polished rock of granite and marble that formed the walls. Their perfectly ordered reason—their ability to think rationally and avoid lies, temptation, and sin—was the perfectly formed mortar that held the rocks together. Satan knew that he couldn't attack the rocks of truth, so he used emotion and imagination to affect Adam and Eve's perception. Original Sin created a crack in the mortar that held the rocks together. It was a small crack, but it was still a weakness that they passed along throughout the generations that came after them.

After Satan realized he couldn't stop the spread of Christianity, he looked back at where he had been successful in the past and realized that the crack in our reason and our ability to think and perceive clearly could be further exploited. Even though Baptism washes away Original Sin and infuses us with virtue, we still have that inherited weakness toward sin. Now that he had identified that weakness in the mortar of right reason, Satan planted the ivy of misperception around the Domestic Church, the house of faith formed by marriage. He knew that over time, the ivy of misperception would grow up the walls, attaching itself to the house. Some people would like how the ivy looked, and they would let it grow. What would be hidden, however, was the damage the ivy of misperception was doing to the house.

## ROOTS ENTER THE CRACKS

Long before Johannes Gutenberg invented the printing press, there was a Franciscan friar named William of Ockham. Born in London, England, in 1285, William of Ockham is most widely known for the philosophical theory that bears his name: Ockham's Razor. But he is less widely known for his theological theories that laid a foundation for people who followed him. William of Ockham separated religion and reason and taught that human reason cannot prove the immortality of the soul, nor could it prove the existence or the infinite nature of God. He argued that the nature of anything of this world could be ascertained only by what we can perceive with our senses and that anything theological could only be known by faith. He also taught that God's laws are not created by His intellect but by His will alone. What he taught stood in direct opposition to the doctrines of Church Fathers and Doctors of the Church, most notably St. Thomas Aquinas's work on faith and reason.

St. Thomas Aquinas used a very practical and well-reasoned scholastic approach of thesis and antithesis to explain theological concepts. This approach was used by all the well-known scholastics before him, such as Aristotle. This method was exhibited in his *Summa Theologica*. The first step is to ask the question about the issue to be considered. The antithesis answers are then listed; these are the "wrong answers" to the question. Then the thesis answers are listed; these are the proposed "right answers" to the question. Finally, each of the antithesis answers is strongly refuted to show that only the thesis answer can be the correct answer. This method relied strictly on logic and reason. Ockham's work gave rise to a new way of thinking that relied on only what can be observed by our senses and abandoned the reasoned, logical approach. The old way of the scholastic method—called the *via antiqua*—was cast aside for the new way, the *via moderna*.

William of Ockham's work was like a small earthquake that created more cracks in the mortar of right reason and fractured the work of over 1300 years of his predecessors, work that is still affirmed as truth to this very day. A synod of bishops found Ockham's teachings to be highly unorthodox, and William of Ockham was summoned by a papal court in 1324 to defend himself against charges of heresy. But the damage was already done. In the cracks formed by William of Ockham, the ivy of misperception began to take more roots, opening wider the fractures for other roots to enter and continue to split the mortar of right reason. Philosophers began to adopt this new way of thinking: the Nominalists, as they are called, included John Buridan, Pierre d'Ailly, Gregory of Rimini, and later, Gabriel Biel. At the same time, others such as Marsilius of Padua, John Wycliffe, and Jan Hus would use the same Ockhamist approaches to attack long-standing theological teachings of the Church. Collectively, the work of these people would influence a whole new generation of theological thinkers and be crucial in setting the stage for Satan's full-blown attack on both the Church and the Domestic Church.

# V. THE GROWING DIVIDE

"These are the ones who cause divisions;
they live on the natural plane,
devoid of the Spirit."
JUDE 1:19

G OD works with broken people all the time to do His holy work. Moses murdered an Egyptian in cold blood, fled to the desert, then returned to lead the Israelites out of Egypt. David committed adultery and murder, then went on to establish the House of David from which the Messiah would come. Simon was brash, zealous, and denied Christ three times *after* Christ renamed him Peter and gave him the keys to Heaven. Then during the days of the early Church, while Peter's teachings were infallible, his conduct at times showed signs of the old, worldly Simon who had to be rebuked by Paul. Some things, as the saying goes, never change.

## IN NAME ONLY, PART I

The Middle Ages marked a time of great turbulence in the Church. Toward the end of that time period, due to shifting political powers, the papacy moved from Rome, to Avignon, France, then back to Rome. Shortly after re-settling the papacy in Rome, the Schism of 1378 saw three men driven by politics, money, and power each claim to be pope, and then excommunicate each other. Fighting between regional kingdoms and the politics of the time meant that Pope Boniface IX found himself paying both mercenaries and bribes. To make these payments, he began a series of actions to which even his supporters objected. He auctioned off leases for land that the Church owned, sold open office positions within the Curia, and began the practice of selling indulgences. By the time of his death in 1404, the papacy was bankrupt, and the Church was deeply divided. His successor, Pope Innocent VII, saw riots, murder, and chaos during his two-year reign, then he himself died under mysterious circumstances. The Schism finally ended in 1417, but damage to the respectability of the papal office and its authority had already been done.

Even after the end of the Schism, the stewardship of Christ's Church seemed to come second to the worldly affairs of some popes. Between adjusting to ever-changing political winds, maintaining personal agendas, confronting direct attacks against the legitimacy of the papacy, fending off attacks in the east by the Turks and the Ottoman Empire, and the Black Plague, the next century turned the eyes of the popes away from their pastoral duties and toward themselves and other affairs.

As the 15th Century drew to a close in Renaissance Italy, Pope Sixtus IV turned a blind eye to the ecclesiastical abuses and the conduct of the Curia. Instead, he spent lavishly on many projects. He built a fleet of boats to help the war effort against the Turks while paving every street in Rome, something that had never been done in the history of the city. He also took the opportunity to help out scores of his relatives, making them cardinals or giving them high-paying jobs. His successors Innocent VIII, Alexander VI, Pius III, and Julius II fared no better. The teaching office of the papacy had been virtually abandoned and the spiritual guidance of the Church was at times completely absent. The popes' appointment of totally unqualified relatives to ecclesiastical positions like the cardinalate resulted in a total degeneration of the Curia, as these people engaged in every sort of blasphemy and scandal. Yet the survival of the Church during this era truly proves the promise of Christ that when it comes to His Church, "the gates of the netherworld shall not prevail against it." Only by the protection of Jesus Christ and the providence of God would the Church be able to survive this time and what was to come, which would be far worse than mere scandal. Just as God uses broken people to do good and holy things, Satan uses broken people too, he just uses them to create more broken people.

### FAULT LINE

Into this tumultuous time, a copper miner named Hans and his wife Margarethe gave birth to their first child, a son, on 10 November, 1483, in Eiselben, Saxony. The child was baptized the next day on the feast day of St. Martin of Tours, and so his parents named him Martin. Hans wanted Martin to be a lawyer, paid for his son's schooling, and eventually sent him off to the University of Erfurt in 1501 at the age of 19. Martin received his master's degree four years later. He then followed his father's wishes for him to attend law school there, but dropped out within a year, much to his father's dismay. Young Martin was despondent, clinically depressed, and uncertain about what to do with his life. He quickly found that he had no pleasure in the law or in philosophy. His tutors, Bartholomaeus Arnoldi von Usingen and Jodocus Trutfetter, both of whom he highly respected, taught him to be suspicious of even the greatest philosophers and theologians. On 2 July 1505, he was riding on horseback during a thunderstorm when a lightning bolt struck nearby. Terrified, he cried out, "Help! Saint Anne, I will become a monk!" (Saint Anne is the patron saint of miners and likely someone revered by Martin's devout family.) Fifteen days later, with no prior draw toward religious life, Martin Luther joined a closed Augustinian cloister in Erfurt.

After entering the Augustinian order, Martin threw himself into his studies. Martin Luther biographer and historian Preserved Smith wrote in *The Life and Letters of Martin Luther*:

*"The theologians he read belonged to what was then called 'the modern' school— 'the modernists' of the sixteenth century. Thomas Aquinas, perhaps the greatest of the schoolmen, was not much regarded; he belonged to the old-fashioned, superseded faction. The philosopher most studied was William Occam [sic]; next to him Gabriel Biel, the Parisian doctors Ailly and Gerson, Bernard of Clairvaux, Bonaventura, John Mauburn, and Gerhard of Zütphen. The fundamental thesis of the Occamists [sic] was that man can do anything he will—fulfill the Ten Commandments to the letter or persuade his reason that white is black. The cloister adopted this view and held that by a man's own acts, asceticism, prayer, and meditation, he could prepare his soul for union with God. Biel especially emphasized the possibility and duty of a man hating his own sins; —fear, said he, is not enough to make repentance acceptable to God."*[38]

In addition to being steeped in this theology, a key component to Augustinian spirituality at the time was the concept of *massa damnata*, which is the premise originating from St. Augustine that the majority of people will not be saved. While no one questions that Luther excelled in his studies, what is clear from his writings of the period is that he still did not find peace in his troubled heart. His despondency and depression only grew worse as his doubts grew ever greater about his own salvation.

The depression that haunted him his entire life likely stemmed from his relationship with his father, Hans Luther. From boyhood, Martin could never seem to please his father, who one time whipped young Martin so severely that he ran away from home. As Martin Luther historian Ken Hensley points out, "Now, it's clear that Luther loved his mother and father and understood that what they had done they had done with good intentions. But it's also clear, and anyone reading Luther's life will see this, that his experiences growing up—and in a special way his relationship with his father—contributed to struggles he had with depression throughout his life. I believe this also had a tremendous effect on how Luther viewed God."[39] Reading accounts of Luther's life in his own words, a clear parallel emerges: he felt like he was never good enough to please his earthly father, and he used the same language to describe his relationship with God the Father; in short, he felt like he could never please either one. All earthly fathers are called to be a model of God the Father to their children, and Martin Luther's perception of *both* fathers became one of someone who was exacting, cruel, and impossible to please no matter how hard he tried. Martin Luther was not just a wounded man, but a man with such deep spiritual wounds that he hated God and God's justice. Martin Luther's faulty perception of God the Father was the lever Satan would lean upon.

Luther said, "I greatly longed to understand Paul's Epistle to the Romans and nothing stood in the way but that one expression, 'the justice of God,' because I took it to mean that justice whereby God is just and deals justly in punishing the unjust. My situation was that, although an impeccable monk, I stood before God as a sinner troubled in conscience, and I had no confidence that my merit would assuage him. Therefore I did not love a just and angry God, but rather hated and murmured against him."[40] "I lost touch with Christ the Savior and Comforter, and made of him the jailer and hangman of my poor soul."[41] "I was more than once driven to the very abyss of despair so that I wished I had never been created. Love God? I hated him!"[42] Biographer Preserved Smith observed, "God appeared to him as a cruel judge; he felt that he could never do enough to win his favor and deserve free pardon."[43] Aware of Martin's spiritual depression, his friend, mentor, confessor, and vicar general of the Augustinian order Johann von Staupitz famously said to him, "God is not angry with you. It is you who are angry with God! Don't you know that God commands you to hope?"[44]

It was Luther's perception that if God's laws seem too cumbersome or difficult to follow, then it meant that God is just angry and mean and impossible to please. His theology continued to evolve over time, eventually reaching the development of his idea of being saved by faith alone (Sola Fide) around 1508 or 1509 (his accounts are unclear as to the exact year), thanks in large part to the via moderna in general, and William of Ockham in particular. Martin Luther called Ockham "his 'dear teacher,' and declared himself to be of Ockham's party—sum Occamicae factionis.[45] Among the teachings of Ockham was the concept of fideism, the view that God's existence cannot be proven by logic and is a matter of faith alone. This stood contrary to St. Thomas Aquinas, who offered not one but five logical proofs in his renowned scholastic work, the Summa Theologiae. Further, Ockham's heretical works claimed that God's laws are not created by His intellect but by His will alone, so therefore, God can do whatever He wants to do. Using Ockham's principles, Luther took this to the next logical conclusion: if God uses

His power without being bound by His intellect that means He can save anyone for whatever reason He feels like. And *that* means you can be saved by faith alone. The anguish in Luther's heart had found soothing relief in a lie, that it doesn't matter what your works are so long as you have faith. In Luther's new interpretation, one need not detest their sins and try to avoid sin since mere faith in salvation was enough to guarantee it. Finally, Martin Luther found the father he always wanted in the form of an alternate Heavenly Father who, in Luther's words, has a "fatherly, friendly heart, in which there is no anger nor ungraciousness."[46]

In 1510 or 1511 (again, his accounts are unclear as to the exact year), Martin Luther left Wittenberg for Rome with another monk to attend to official business of their order, with Martin serving as the junior traveling companion of the more senior monk. He was excited to make the trip and planned to make a general confession of all his sins and receive absolution.[47] He was so enlivened at this opportunity that upon reaching their destination, he reportedly fell on his face and cried out, "Hail, holy Rome!" But when he got there, he was shocked at what he saw: "Rome is a harlot. I would not take a thousand gulden not to have seen it, for I never would have believed the true state of affairs from what other people told me, had I not seen it myself. The Italians mocked us for being pious monks, for they hold Christians fools. They say six or seven masses in the time it takes me to say one, for they take money for it and I do not. The only crime in Italy is poverty. They still punish homicide and theft a little, for they have to, but no other sin is too gross for them.... So great and bold is Roman impiety that neither God nor man, neither sin nor shame, is feared. All good men who have seen Rome bear witness to this; all bad ones come back worse than before."[48]

Disillusioned, Martin returned to Wittenberg with the other monk after their business in Rome was finished. Shortly after returning to the monastery, von Staupitz told Martin that he wanted him to begin working on his doctorate in Sacred Scripture so that he could assume the chair of biblical theology at the University of Wittenberg. Von Staupitz thought that if Martin devoted himself to studying Scripture that it would help him out of his depression.[49] In 1513, Martin received his doctorate and began lecturing at the University of Wittenberg. What he saw in Rome continued to haunt him, however, and the continued secular scandals committed by the papacy under Pope Leo X were an increasing problem. Martin took particular issue with the selling of indulgences, which had only gotten worse under the new pope. Here he was, starving himself through fasting to the point people could see his bones, freezing himself cold in his room at night, and doing all sorts of other mortifications for his sinfulness, while the laity were simply buying indulgences that were supposed to get them out of paying for their sins in Purgatory. People were putting more faith in their paid-for indulgence than they were in being actually penitent for their sins. For several months in early 1517, Martin preached against the purchase of indulgences and exhorted the need for repentance.

He began to assemble a list of statements that he wanted to open to academic discussion. While at this point he affirmed that Purgatory must exist and that indulgences were a valid practice, he objected to how they were currently being handled. He wrote his list of "95 Theses" in Latin (the common formal language of educators at the time), and in the heading, invited interested scholars from other cities to participate in a formal discussion. What happened next is debated by historians, biographers, and academics. Some say Luther defiantly nailed the "95 Theses" to the door of All Saints' Church in Wittenberg; statutes at Wittenberg at the time called for *any* theses calling for academic debate to be posted to the door of every church in the city; Luther himself always claimed he raised his objections through proper channels. What is known as fact is that on 31 October 1517, Luther wrote a letter to his archbishop to alert him of the pastoral problems he was running into regarding the sale of indulgences and included a copy of his "95 Theses." From there, how the "95 Theses" got translated into German and distributed remains a bit of an historical mystery. But no one can debate the fallout.

Martin Luther was right that the Catholic Church had major problems. Historian Hilaire Belloc noted, "No one can deny that the evils provoking reform in the Church were deep rooted and widespread. They threatened the very life of Christendom itself. All who thought at all about what was going on around them realized how perilous things were and how great was the need of reform."[50] While Luther's identification of the problems was never in question, his *solutions* to the problems were what the Church has always disagreed with.*

### AND THE IVY GREW AND GREW

In Martin Luther, a spiritually deeply injured man with a distorted perception of God's justice who was heavily influenced by the Nominalists' writings of the *via moderna*, Satan had found his first major influential voice. Heresies that had been struck down and driven out of the Church a thousand years earlier suddenly found new life. Research into the writings of Luther just before his infamous "95 Theses" reveals that "when he made his attack on Catholic theology, [he] had no knowledge of the great scholastics, including St. Thomas Aquinas. His theological reading had not extended beyond the disciples of Occam [sic]; Gabriel Biel had been his most familiar author."[51]

* Many of Luther's critiques were in fact quite valid, and the Catholic Church admitted as much, though it took a few decades for Pope Adrian VI to finally admit: "We know that for years there have been many abominable offenses in spiritual matters and violations of the Commandments committed at this Holy See, yes, that everything has in fact been perverted. ... The first thing that must be done is to reform the Curia, the origin of all the evil." Ultimately, this would take another century and six popes before the reforms took hold at the Council of Trent.

# V. The Growing Divide

Luther then began disagreeing with Church teachings on everything from free will (saying that no one had the free will to be able to overcome sinful behaviors) to good works (saying that there's no such thing as a good work.) He was no longer just disagreeing with the Pope and taking issue with the conduct of the Curia; *he was disagreeing with fundamental teachings of 1500 years of Christianity.*

A few months after the "95 Theses," Luther began to have to defend his statements and writings. Initially, Luther clung to his Catholic faith. In July 1518 he still believed that "the Roman Church has always maintained the true faith, and that it is necessary for all Christians to be in unity of faith with her."[52] This was to change, however, as he refused to admit any error at all in any of his theological beliefs that differed from the teachings of the Catholic Church. Still troubled by his experience in Rome, he went on to attack the Church itself. Though he was an Augustinian friar, and he studied the works of St. Augustine devoutly, Martin ignored this saint and founder of his order who said not to blame the Church for the conduct of bad Christians. A thousand years earlier, St. Augustine stated, "My advice to you now is this: that you should at least desist from slandering the Catholic Church, by declaiming against the conduct of men whom the Church herself condemns, seeking daily to correct them as wicked children."[53]

Martin Luther was nothing if not industrious, publishing 25 books in addition to other pamphlets and documents prior to his trial for heresy. One of these works was "The Babylonian Captivity of the Church," published in 1520, which reduced the seven Sacraments down to two. About the Sacrament of Marriage, in particular, Luther said, "Not only is marriage regarded as a sacrament without the least warrant of Scripture, but the very ordinances which extol it as a sacrament have turned it into a farce.... Nowhere do we read that the man who marries a wife receives any grace of God. There is not even a divinely instituted sign in marriage, nor do we read anywhere that marriage was instituted by God to be a sign of anything."[54] Luther was also flexible on reasons for divorce, making it justifiable for just about anyone with a problem with their spouse. He went on to also approve of bigamy, most notably approving of the bigamous marriage of Prince Phillip of Hesse, saying that it was preferable to divorce and nowhere in Scripture was it disallowed. As if that wasn't enough, Luther completely removed the Church's role in marriage, giving that authority to the secular governments. It was no longer something made by and sacred to God but rather a matter of paperwork handled at city hall.

Luther's ignorance of the works of Church Fathers becomes clear when one compares his views on marriage and divorce with those of Bishop Asterius of Amasea, who served the Church 1100 years before Martin Luther:

*"For, behold, marriage, the chief affair of human life, is regulated by [God], and the limits of this union and the conditions of its dissolution are exactly determined.... 'The creation itself,' says [the Lord], 'shows its aim to be union, not separation.' The Creator was the first bestower of the bride in marriage, since he joined the first human beings in the marriage bond, giving to those who should come after, the inflexible ordinance of the conjugal life, which must be recognized as the law of God; and they who are thus associated with one another are no longer two, but one flesh, so that 'What God hath joined together, let not man put asunder.' ... For it is not as in the case of mistresses, a companionship for a few days only, nor a mere quest for pleasure, but like most other things is subject to rule and regulation. But in marriage, O man, both soul and body are united, so that disposition is mingled with disposition, and flesh with flesh. How, then, are you going to sever the bond of marriage without suffering? How can you withdraw from this union easily and without pain, after taking your sister and wife not as a servant of a few days, but as a partner for life, a sister by reason of her formation and creation,—for you were both made of the same element of earth and of the same substance,—and wife because of the conjugal union, because of the law of marriage? If, then, the*

*woman you have lightly divorced shall take the book of Genesis and drag you unto the Judge, who is both Judge and witness, tell me, what will you say? How will you repudiate your own utterance which you made in the name of God, which Moses, the servant of God, recorded, instead of some cheap notary?"* [55]

The charges against Luther were summed up thus: "He has sullied marriage, disparaged confession, and denied the body and blood of our Lord. He makes the sacraments depend on the faith of the recipient. He is pagan in his denial of free will. This devil in the habit of a monk has brought together ancient errors into one stinking puddle and has invented new ones. He denies the power of the keys and encourages the laity to wash their hands in the blood of the clergy. His teaching makes for rebellion, division, war, murder, robbery, arson, and the collapse of Christendom.... We have labored with him, but he recognizes only the authority of Scripture, *which he interprets in his own sense.*"[56] (Emphasis added.) Eventually after several rounds of debates and trials for heresy, he was excommunicated on 3 January 1521.

After breaking from the Catholic Church, Luther set to work on his own German translation of the Bible. The Bible used by the Church at the time was the Latin Vulgate, which was compiled by St. Jerome between 383 and 405 AD under orders from Pope Damasus I to unify the Biblical canon. Its 80 books existed unchanged, until Martin Luther. From the existing German translations of the Bible, Luther removed seven books and parts of two others. He called the Epistle of James "an epistle full of straw," and would have removed it, Esther, and the Apocalypse were it not for the advice of some of his closest friends. Anything that went against his new perception of Christianity was edited or removed outright.

*"But even for the books he chose to retain, he showed little or no respect. Here are some examples of his judgments on them. Of the Pentateuch [the first five books of the Bible] he says: 'We have no wish either to see or hear Moses.' ... 'Of*

*very little worth is the book of Baruch, whoever the worthy Baruch may be.'
'Esdras I would not translate, because there is nothing in it which you might
not find better in Aesop.' 'Job spoke not as it stands written in his book; but
only had such thoughts. It is merely the argument of a fable. It is probable that
Solomon wrote and made this book.' ... 'The book of Esther I toss into the Elbe.
I am such an enemy to the book of Esther that I wish it did not exist, for it
Judaizes too much and has in it a great deal of heathenish naughtiness.' 'The
history of Jonah is so monstrous that it is absolutely incredible.' 'The first book
of the Maccabees might have been taken into the Scriptures, but the second is
rightly cast out, though there is some good in it.' ... In a word, as is admitted
by a recent Protestant writer: 'Luther has no fixed theory of inspiration: if all
his works suppose the inspiration of the Sacred Writings, all his conduct shows
that he makes himself the supreme judge of it.'" [57]*

*"As a proof of the arbitrary spirit which Luther showed in making his
translation of the Bible, we have the fact that he confessed to have added, for
dogmatic reasons, the word 'alone' to the text of St. Paul (Romans 3:28):—
'Therefore we conclude that a man is justified by faith without the deeds of
the law.' Luther rendered the passage 'by faith alone'; and when reproached
for this, he wrote:—'You tell me what a great fuss the Papists are making
because the word "alone" is not in the text of Paul. If your Papist makes such
an unnecessary row about the word "alone," say right out to him:—"Dr.
Martin Luther* will have it so," and say:—"Papists and asses are one and the
same thing." I will have it so, and I order it to be so, and my will is
reason enough. I know very well that the word "alone" is not in the Latin
and Greek text, and it was not necessary for the Papists to teach me that. It
is true, those letters are not in it, which letters the jackasses look at, as a cow
stares at a new gate. ... It ["alone"] shall remain in my New Testament, and
if all the Popish donkeys were to get mad and beside themselves, they will not
get it out.'" [58]*

Luther's revisions to the Bible were so bad that in 1836, "many Lutheran
consistories called for its entire revision." [59]

Of course, it was Luther's work that formed the basis of the Protestant Reformation. As Hilaire Belloc noted, "The Protestant attack differed from the rest especially in this characteristic, that its attack did not consist in the promulgation of a new doctrine or of a new authority, that it made no concerted attempt at creating a counter-Church, but had for its principle the *denial of unity*. It was an effort to promote that state of mind in which a Church in the old sense of the word—that is, an infallible, united, teaching body, a Person speaking with Divine authority—should be denied; not the doctrines it might happen to advance, but its very claim to advance them with *unique authority*." [60] (Emphasis added.) The irony is that in breaking away from the Catholic Church in part because of the unique authority of the Papacy, Martin Luther set himself up as the unique authority on the denial of unique authority. Yes, it's a logical brain twister.

In 1524, a mere three years after Luther was excommunicated from the Catholic Church, the Peasant's War broke out in Germany, fueled in part by Reformationist ideals. Tens of thousands were killed. Elsewhere, factions of Reformationism began to take root: Zwingli and John Calvin gave birth to the Reformed Reformationist movement that broke from the Magisterial Reformationist movement started by Martin Luther. Then came the Radical Reformationists. Later, the Anglicans. It didn't take long for Luther to see clearly the evil that he had started. In a letter he wrote in 1525 he lamented, "The devil seeing that this sort [sic] of disturbances could not last, has devised a new one; and begins to rage in his members, I mean in the ungodly, through whom he makes his way in all sorts of chimerical follies and extravagant doctrines. This won't have baptism, that denies the efficacy of the Lord's supper; a third puts a world between this and the last judgement; others teach that Jesus Christ is not God; some say this, others that; and there are almost as many sects and beliefs as there are heads.... When the pope reigned we heard nothing of these troubles." [61] But it was too late to stop what Martin Luther had begun.

The multitude of divisions introduced with the Protestant Reformation would eventually result in more than just Christ's Church being divided between the Catholic Church and Protestants. Now, with everyone being given the "freedom" to interpret Scripture as they saw fit, using their own unique perception of what it means to be a Christian, the Protestant denominations themselves would further be divided, subdivided, and splintered into over 47,000 denominations worldwide as of this writing.[62] As Jesus said, "And if a house is divided against itself, that house will not be able to stand."[63] It should be noted that the denomination that bears Luther's name—the Lutheran Church—has itself divided into over 40 denominations in North America alone. What's more, that which Luther had claimed should be the basis of faith—Scripture alone *(Sola Scriptura)*—was now a point of division rather than unity. As G.K. Chesterton observed, "The Bible by itself cannot be a basis of agreement when it is a cause of disagreement; it cannot be the common ground of Christians when some take it allegorically and some literally."

Rather than being mastered *by* faith and allowing God to rule him, Luther became the master *of* his faith, a faith of his own making and of his own understanding. And in so doing, he told everyone who followed him that they too had the ability to become *their* own masters. Through Martin Luther, Satan used his old playbook: Create doubt about truth. Create fear about everything good. Take everything beautiful and distort and disfigure it with lies. Cause us to question our perception about what is good and what is evil, what is truth and what is falsehood.

The Protestant Reformation is widely regarded as the beginning of "The Age of Enlightenment," also known as "The Age of Reason." Philosophers would replace theologians as the "big thinkers" in society, circulating their ideas at meetings of groups and publishing pamphlets or tracts. Their theories replaced truths about God and His teachings with man-made "reason." Each philosopher gained a following, and as these followers allowed the lies of Satan to corrupt their hearts and minds and perceptions, each unwittingly became another one of Satan's helpers. They didn't know that they were helping Satan accomplish his goals; they just liked what they heard or what they read. It made sense to them in some way, justified their behavior, or it just made them feel good. The Enlightenment sought to create a society of morality uncoupled from religion—not just Christianity, but *any* religion. In so doing, it sought to make man the highest authority of morality. The result has been cascading waves of relativism that have eroded away the morality that formed the bedrock of society, morality that once came from religion.

We are supposed to be strengthened by our unity in faith, but instead, Satan created a *perpetual* situation in which man's faulty perception is left to question truth, fear what is good, and believe lies that distort the beauty of Christ's Church. And note here the subtlety of Satan: people for generations would go on to become unwitting pawns, *completely* unaware of the damage they would ultimately cause to both Christ's Church and the Domestic Church by causing other people to question *their* perceptions of the true, the good, and the beautiful. Satan no longer has to do the heavy lifting because *we're doing it for him.* The Reformation ushered in an era with weakened walls of *absolute truth*, and the resulting infighting between Christians started moving all of society toward a weakened state. Without those walls of absolute truth to keep Satan out, his whispered question, "What is truth?" became much more powerful.

While God permits such evil to tempt and test us, in His infinite love for us, He also provides for us an advocate for our salvation.

# VI. The Woman and The Serpent

"We, then, have strayed from the way of truth,
and the light of righteousness did not shine for us,
and the sun did not rise for us.

We were entangled in the thorns of mischief and of ruin;
we journeyed through trackless deserts,
but the way of the Lord we never knew."

Wisdom 5:6-7

MOST everyone has stories about his mother warning him repeatedly about things that could hurt him. There's an endless list of things moms worry about: Getting too close to the road, strangers, playing with knives, going too high on the swings, driving too recklessly, hanging out with and dating the wrong people, and on and on. Most people can recount a seemingly endless list of their mother's worries. But skinned knees and broken hearts are much less worrisome than an eternity in Hell. In God's enduring love for us, He has given every one of us a perfect mother whose only worry is our salvation.

### BEHOLD, YOUR MOTHER

In I Kings 2:12, Solomon, son of David, is anointed King of Israel. In verse 19, we see Solomon issue a decree for a throne to be placed at his right hand for "The Queen Mother" ("Gebirah" in Hebrew). She gave him counsel, wisdom, and instruction based on her experience. From that point on, the Davidic Dynasty, which existed for over 400 years, always had a Queen Mother, and the title is used at least five times in the Old Testament.[64] When we study scriptural accounts of the role of the Queen Mother, we know that people would bring her their requests in hopes that her intercession on their behalf would help them gain favor from the king. While the king retained ultimate decision-making authority, the role of the Queen Mother was an important one.

Since Jesus is born in the line of David (Luke 1:27, 32) to fulfill Scripture as the King of Israel (II Samuel 7:16; 23:5), then in keeping with Jewish tradition, Mary is the Queen Mother. As we know, Jesus' kingdom was not just limited to Israel and the Jews, and the years He was with us on earth; His kingdom is both in Heaven and on earth, over both Jew and Gentile, and it will last forever. So Mary's role as Queen Mother also extends throughout both Heaven and on earth, for both Jew and Gentile, forever. We see this pronouncement from the cross at Calvary: Jesus turned to Mary and John the Apostle, and "he said to his mother, 'Woman, behold, your son.' Then he said to the disciple,

'Behold, your mother.'"[65] This is an important event in Scripture because it tells us two things.

First, it proves that Jesus was the only child of Mary. Joseph is agreed upon to have been dead for some time, so by Jewish law, it was the responsibility of the eldest son to take care of his mother. We know that Jesus was the firstborn of Mary according to the gospels of both St. Luke (2:7) and St. Matthew (1:25) so that responsibility would fall to Jesus. According to Jewish law, if the firstborn were to die before the widowed mother, the responsibility of the mother would fall to the next eldest brother. If there were no other brothers, it would fall to the family of the eldest sister. Jesus was the fulfillment of the law (Matthew 5:17), and He was a perfect Jew in all regards. He could not give his mother to St. John to care for and still keep the law if he had blood siblings.

Second, this pronouncement by Jesus gave Mary not just to St. John but to all mankind. When Jesus assumed His throne, Mary became our perpetual mother in Heaven, our Queen Mother. And like every mother, she cares for her children. Our Heavenly Mother worries about us even more than our earthly mothers do, but her list of worries is much shorter. In fact, it contains only one thing: sin. Out of her love for us and her desire for us all to attain salvation, she has repeatedly tried to warn us by visiting us through apparitions.

### HALF A WORLD AWAY

While Europe was undergoing religious and political upheaval, a group of nuns from Spain set sail for South America to found a convent. Among them was Mother Mariana de Jesus Torres. They arrived in Quito, Ecuador, on 30 December, 1576, and on 13 January 1577, the convent was officially established with seven nuns in the cloister. Among them, "Mariana was already a mystic, favored with visions, especially of Our Lady and Our Lord."[66] The first apparition to Mother Mariana appeared on 2 February 1594.* Several apparitions and other miracles happened at the convent in Quito over the next 40 years. "When she first appeared to the nun, our Blessed Mother showed herself as the Sorrowful Virgin, weeping as Christ suffered His death agony on the cross. She made known that this anguish was 'for the criminal world'—specifically for the heresy, blasphemy and impurity of the 20th century." [67]

During the apparition of 21 January 1610, Mary said to Mother Mariana:

*"... from the end of the 19th century and from shortly after the middle of the 20th century ... the passions will erupt and there will be a total corruption of customs, for Satan will reign almost completely by means of the Masonic Sects. They will focus principally on the children in order to sustain this general corruption. Woe to the children of these times! It will be difficult to receive the Sacrament of Baptism and also the Sacrament of Confirmation. They will receive the Sacrament of Confession only if they remain in Catholic schools, for the Devil will make a great effort to destroy it through persons in position [sic] of authority. The same thing will happen with the Sacrament of Holy Communion. Alas! How deeply I grieve to manifest to you the many enormous sacrileges—both public as well as secret—that will occur from profanation of the Holy Eucharist. Often, during this epoch the enemies of Jesus Christ, instigated by the Devil, will steal consecrated Hosts from the churches so that they might profane the Eucharistic Species. My Most Holy Son will see Himself cast upon the ground and trampled upon by filthy feet." [68]*

* The Catholic Church doesn't take apparitions lightly and thoroughly investigates each one, erring on the side of skepticism. This is necessary because Sacred Scripture tells us that "even Satan masquerades as an angel of light," and it would be better to believe no apparition rather than believe a false one. Only after a rigorous investigation is a particular apparition listed as "worthy of belief," and sometimes the investigation into an alleged apparition has taken over 100 years. No Catholic is ever bound to believe them.

*"As for the Sacrament of Matrimony, which symbolizes the union of Christ with His Church, it will be attacked and profaned in the fullest sense of the word. Masonry, which will then be in power, will enact iniquitous laws with the objective of doing away with this Sacrament, making it easy for everyone to live in sin, encouraging the procreation of illegitimate children born without the blessing of the Church. The Christian spirit will rapidly decay, extinguishing the precious light of Faith until it reaches the point that there will be an almost total and general corruption of customs.... Moreover, in these unhappy times, there will be unbridled luxury which, acting thus to snare the rest into sin, will conquer innumerable frivolous souls who will be lost. Innocence will almost no longer be found in children, nor modesty in women, and in this supreme moment of need of the Church, those who should speak will fall silent."* [69]

On 2 February 1634, forty years to the day of the first apparition, Mother Mariana was at Eucharistic adoration and noticed that the sanctuary lamp had burned out. Mary appeared to her and told her that this was a sign with several meanings:

*"[T]oward the end of the nineteenth century and throughout a great part of the twentieth many heresies will be propagated in these lands.... the precious light of faith will be extinguished in souls because of an almost total corruption of customs.... [T]he lamp was extinguished because of the poisoned atmosphere of impurity which will reign at that time like a filthy sea. It will flow through the streets, squares and public places with such an astonishing lack of restraint that there will be almost no virgin souls left in the world. It is well-known that the vice of impurity extinguishes the light of faith... [T]he power of sects and their ability to penetrate homes and families, thus destroying the beauty of innocence in the hearts of children."* [70]

How unbelievable this must have sounded then: Eucharistic sacrileges, matrimony attacked and profaned, the decline of the Christian spirit; in the 17th century, who outside of the most devout would have taken this message seriously? In particular, what was that about Masonic sects taking power?

### In Name Only, Part II

In 1750, King Joseph I of Portugal appointed Sebastiano José de Carvalho to the position of Marquis de Pombal or Minister of Foreign Affairs. (For simplicity's sake, we'll just refer to him as "Pombal" from here on out.) It didn't take long before it became clear that Pombal was the real power behind the throne. It also didn't take long before he began finding himself at odds with the Society of Jesus, also known as the Jesuits, whom he saw as too powerful and, at the same time, through their moral guidance, too limiting to the economic growth of Portugal in the colonies in the Americas.

Portugal was predominantly a Catholic nation, and the Jesuits had a strong influence on the country and its policies both at home and abroad. From running the schools to advising the king on politics, the presence of the Jesuits was everywhere. Despite its outward religious appearance, however, Lisbon was sinful at its core. Mark Molesky, author of *This Gulf of Fire* writes, "By the eighteenth century, the distinction between Lisbon's convents and its brothels was practically nonexistent.... 'The sin which the Portuguese acknowledge to be the most heinous,' wrote one French traveler, 'is that of the flesh; and it is precisely the one into which they rush with the greatest impetuosity.' ... Most upper-class women dressed seductively in eighteenth-century Lisbon, favoring velvet corsets and silk neckerchiefs that exposed their cleavage.... around their necks they wore a ribbon or choker with a gold cross that dangled suggestively between their breasts."[71] Vice was as prevalent as crucifixes, and with it came crime and regular murders. In eighteenth-century Lisbon, no sin was too great nor committed too frequently. Obviously, they suffered from a faulty perception of God.

On the morning of 1 November 1755, a great earthquake struck Lisbon while many Catholics were attending Mass to celebrate All Saint's Day. The quake lasted for about six minutes and could be felt as far away as Africa to the south and Finland to the north. The quake created tsunamis in the ocean as high as 66 feet that hit North Africa, and even swept across the Atlantic, hitting Martinique, Barbados, and even Brazil. The water that was sucked away from Lisbon as part of the tsunami came rushing back some 40 minutes later, flooding the city and carrying some of the earthquake survivors out to sea. The calamity didn't end there, as candles lit in churches and homes for All Saint's Day were knocked over and started massive fires all over the city. When it was all over, an estimated 30-40,000 people were killed in Lisbon alone.

Sixty-six-year-old Father Gabriel Malagrida, one of the Jesuits who was in Lisbon that day, preached to the people a few months afterward: "'Know, oh Lisbon,' he thundered, 'that the destroyers of so many houses and palaces, the devastators of so many churches and monasteries, the killer of so many people ... are not comets, stars, vapors, exhalations, phenomena, accidents, or natural causes—but only our intolerable sins.' Lisbon, he proclaimed, had become a 'Babylon of inconsolable confusion,' which the Good Lord, in His righteous outrage, had chosen to smash to the ground."[72]

Pombal, on the other hand, saw it as an opportunity to rebuild Lisbon, and also reform all of Portugal. He instructed his chief engineer to have his people come up with plans for rebuilding the city. Six plans were generated. It should be noted that "Pombal was a Freemason and that plan 5, which he chose, included Masonic symbols and was developed by Eugénio dos Santos, also a Freemason. According to this line of thought, after the 1755 great tragedy, Lisbon was rebuilt as a huge temple of Freemasonry."[73] In 1759, Pombal kicked the Jesuits out of Portugal completely, and before long the entire country was largely run by Freemasons.

## THE TRUE VINE

Many times, Jesus compared God to someone who owns and supervises work in the fields: the "master of the harvest" (Luke 10:2), "a landowner who planted a vineyard" (Matthew 21:33), and "[a] man [who] planted a vineyard" (Mark 12:1). Perhaps one of most relevant to our discussion comes in John 15, where Jesus said:

*"I am the true vine, and my Father is the vine grower. He takes away every branch in me that does not bear fruit, and every one that does he prunes so that it bears more fruit. You are already pruned because of the word that I spoke to you. Remain in me, as I remain in you. Just as a branch cannot bear fruit on its own unless it remains on the vine, so neither can you unless you remain in me. I am the vine, you are the branches. Whoever remains in me and I in him will bear much fruit, because without me you can do nothing. Anyone who does not remain in me will be thrown out like a branch and wither; people will gather them and throw them into a fire and they will be burned."* [74]

Most interpretations of this passage focus on what happens to branches that are "in" Jesus but which do not bear fruit: the people who claim to follow Christ but who live their lives much differently. Throughout the Gospels, whenever Jesus uses these parables or metaphors of the owner of the vineyard, he speaks of how the owner hires people or gives his servants tasks to complete. They are each rewarded or punished based on the fruits of their labor. Each of us has a mission: to save souls. The Church from its very founding had its marching orders given to it by Jesus: "Go, therefore, and make disciples of all nations, baptizing them in the name of the Father, and of the Son, and of the holy Spirit, teaching them to observe all that I have commanded you." [75] Our job, therefore, is to save souls, and not just our own. God, through His Son Jesus Christ, gave us orders to go save other souls. God's love for mankind is expressed in His mission for us to save as many other people as we can. We who are part of the true vine are all called to bear good fruits and we will all be judged by the fruits we bear.

What is typically overlooked in the passage from John 15 is the phrase "true vine." Note here that Jesus never speaks of who is the false vine. Let us consider that ivy, while beautiful to look at, bears no fruit, nor can it ever bear fruit. The ivy of misperception is, in fact, the false vine. Where Jesus is "the way, and the truth, and the life"[76] that leads souls to Heaven, the ivy of misperception is the false vine, the lie that leads to eternal death.

## THE FALSE VINE

Part of Satan's plan is to weaken the Church by dividing it against itself. The false vine of Satan's lies was growing in and amongst the true vine. The false vine had so entwined itself with the true vine that Christians spent most of their time trying to figure out which was which. The result? Very little fruit to give God, the owner of the vineyard. While Catholics bickered with Protestants about what was truth, and Protestants bickered among themselves about what was truth, the ivy of misperception kept growing. More cracks formed in the mortar of right reason. The walls of the Domestic Church got weaker and weaker.

The growth of heretical ideas, and the groups that believed in them and adopted them, was initially restricted. The spread of these ideas was limited to communications by letter and printing press, and how fast they were distributed was restrained by the speed of horses and sailing ships. But not for long.

## CRITICAL MASS

The time period from 1738 to 1884 was unique in human history. It witnessed the American and French Revolutions, as well as the industrial revolution. The explosion of industry drew people from small farm towns to rapidly-growing cities in pursuit of higher pay. Steam engines were powering boats and trains, allowing people to move more quickly and safely wherever they wanted to go. The electric telegraph, telephone, and invention of the radio sped communications across the oceans and around the world. Brisk movement of not just people but information and ideas was quickly becoming the new way of life. This meant that the swift spreading of Satan's messages would become possible, and as the secular lies spread, more and more people believed them. They unwittingly helped Satan's efforts, and quite unknowingly lost their souls in the process.

In the past Satan had to settle for a tiny crack that influenced and corrupted the hearts and minds of a few dozen here, or maybe a little crack that damned the souls of a hundred or two over there. But now he realized that as the cracks had begun to grow wider and the walls were on the verge of collapse, he would have the ability to reach thousands and soon millions of people all at once. Satan knew that faster travel and electronic communications would help him more rapidly spread his lies. Satan's efforts began to come together and grow at an exponential rate, faster than ever before.

For six hundred years, Satan had been waiting for this: The ivy of misperception he planted had spread completely around the base of the Domestic Church. The roots were deep and embedded in every crack, the vines thick and woody. Just chopping out a vine here and there wouldn't stop his message, and distinguishing between the true vine and the false vine had become almost impossible. The walls of the Domestic Church were weakened, but up until now, the strength of the people inside could patch up the damage and hold up the walls. Satan needed to weaken the people inside. He knew that every time he could get one person to leave the Domestic Church, he could easily bring down everyone left inside it. He would just need to convince people that their Domestic Church wasn't worth saving. Then one by one, the Domestic Churches would be abandoned. Once enough people fled their Domestic Churches, knocking down Christ's Church—which depended upon the unity inside the Domestic Churches—would be no problem at all.

But before all that, he would need to lure people out of their Domestic Churches by offering them a more attractive alternative.

# VII. Building the Alternative

"The sin of the century is the loss of the sense of sin."
Pope Pius XII, 1946

NESTLED in the heart of Rome, a long list of tourist attractions lie footsteps away from each other. If you start your sightseeing journey with a trip to the Colosseum in the morning, a typical route would have you make your way west along the the "Via Papale" or "the Pope's Road," then turn north after lunch at Piazza Navona to finish your day at the Spanish Steps. On your journey, you'll likely stop through the Campo de' Fiori to shop in the open-air market. If you do, you'll see a large statue of a man holding a book with shackled hands, his head covered in a hood, and a scowling, stern look on his face. If you look in the direction of where the statue is looking, you'll realize it is facing the Vatican, which sits only about a mile away across the Tiber River.

The statue is of Giordano Bruno, a Dominican friar who was burned at the stake on that spot by the secular Roman government on Ash Wednesday, 1600, for heresy. Like William of Ockham and Martin Luther, he was gifted with a high level of intelligence, especially his memory skills, which he believed "bestowed some kind of power on those who mastered them."[77] He entered the Dominican monastery at the age of 17, at 24, became a priest, and received the equivalent of a doctorate in theology in 1575 at the age of 27. This wasn't to last long, however. "When a professor ridiculed the Arian heresy (which denies that God is divided into three persons, the doctrine of the Trinity) as 'ignorant,' Bruno defended the rationale of its proponents (if not the heresy itself) and won himself a scolding that he considered unjust and brooded over for years."[78]

This was just the beginning. "He doubted not only the Trinity, but the personhood of God, the divinity of Christ, the Virgin birth and the transubstantiation of the eucharist into the flesh and blood of Christ. He was a universalist, meaning that he believed all of creation (even heathens, unrepentant sinners and demons) would ultimately be reconciled with and forgiven by God, and he apparently believed in reincarnation."[79] By 1576, he was informed that he was being investigated for heresy, so he fled. "To the Church authorities, that was as good as a confession; they defrocked and excommunicated him in absentia."[80]

First he fled to Geneva, then to a long list of cities throughout Europe, including Wittenberg, Frankfurt, Paris, and London. He taught and lectured on logic, philosophy, and metaphysics and published around thirty works, ranging from tracts and pamphlets to a five-hour play. Giordano Bruno never stayed more than two or three years in any one city, typically because he wore out his welcome. After being excommunicated by the Catholic Church, he didn't find a home among Protestants either, being subsequently excommunicated by both the Lutherans and Calvinists. He petitioned on at least three occasions for the Catholic Church to lift his excommunication and was denied each time. "In one of his books, he described himself as 'irritated, recalcitrant, and strange, content with nothing, stubborn as an old man of eighty, skittish as a dog that has been whipped a thousand times.' His nickname, he said, was 'the exasperated.'"[81]

His time wandering through Europe evolved his perception of religion. He developed a personal philosophy and named it "Nolan" after his hometown. Nolan was a combination of the philosophies of St. Thomas Aquinas, Greek philosophers, and Copernicus.[82] He also solidified his heretical beliefs in pantheism: that God is literally in everything, that there is no distinct being that is God, and that mankind's belief in different gods is, in reality, all belief in the same God. Rather than God creating everything, God is everything. So, according to this logic, if God is everything, then God is in us too, and so everyone has the ability to consult their own "inner God" for direction in their lives. As one author noted, for Bruno, "the Messiah has no place. Nor does original sin, or pretty much any sin. God 'makes his sun rise over good and bad,' Bruno wrote. Even devils were going to be pardoned."[83]

Inexplicably, he returned to Italy in 1591, hired by a Venetian nobleman who wanted to be taught Bruno's memory tricks. There was a falling out between Bruno and the nobleman, who turned him over to the Inquisition. Another author noted that ultimately it was "Bruno's 'combative personality' that finally did him in....":

*"[O]ne of Bruno's former cellmates, a man he'd slapped during a dispute and who feared that Bruno had informed on him as well, stepped forward to relate the various blasphemies and heretical convictions Bruno had spouted during their time together behind bars. Their fellow prisoners confirmed that Bruno had cursed God, Christ and the church. Of course, many Italians (then and now) have been known to do this in moments of pique, but the Inquisition also had ample evidence of the philosopher's contempt for friars, Jesuits, scholastics and other church figures (not to mention his very real objections to key Christian doctrines) in his printed works. He had vented as much bile as the most virulent Internet troll, but he was much more eloquent and far from anonymous. Eventually, he ran out of friends and second chances."*[84]

So why did someone erect a statue of a heretic like Giordano Bruno? To answer that, we have to go looking for, as the late great Paul Harvey would say, "the rest of the story."

### SCULPTING IDOLS

The statue was a project started in 1884 by a group of students in Rome who gathered support, financial and otherwise, from some of the most prominent "free thinkers" in Europe at the time: Victor Hugo, Ernest Renan, Ernst Haeckel, and Herbert Spencer to name a few. The sculpture was completed by Ettore Ferrari, a high-ranking member of the *Grande Oriente d'Italia*, an Italian masonic grand lodge formed in 1805, which at one time had broad international influence in the Freemason organization. As it turns out, it was the *Grande Oriente d'Italia* that was behind the movement to erect the statue of Giordano

Bruno. The statue was a response to Pope Leo XIII's 1884 encyclical *Humanum Genus*, which spoke about the evils of Freemasonry.

In the age of the internet there are a lot of crackpot theories about the Freemasons, Illuminati, and other shadowy groups. It is easy to dismiss all talk of Freemasons being evil, and paint everyone who talks about Freemasons with a "conspiracy theorist" brush. For a moment, set those thoughts aside as we will quote public statements that cannot be conspiracies, and show you a bit of history that is far from theory.

Modern Freemasonry is mostly agreed to have started on 24 June 1717, when four Grand Lodges in England joined to become one. Freemasonry can be considered a religion of itself. It has its own oaths, rites, and symbols. It has its own name for God—"The Grand Architect of the Universe"—and its own bible. It describes its own rules for getting to Heaven that do not involve Jesus Christ, and it has its own code of morals. Through its beliefs that there is 1) no absolute truth and 2) no singular monotheistic religion that is the sole deposit of truth, it not only accepts people from all faiths but also encourages them to find and discover their own individual truths. This is, quite simply, an open door through which Satan can enter and create faulty perceptions of what truth is. Oftentimes, his arrival is met with open arms, "for even Satan masquerades as an angel of light" (II Corinthians 11:14). The reason so many Popes over so many years have denounced Freemasonry is because the Freemasons are aligned in total opposition to the Catholic Church, and for years its stated ultimate aim has been the destruction of the Catholic Church as well as *all* of Christianity.

The first Pope to denounce Freemasonry was Pope Clement XII in his Papal Bull *In Eminenti* on 28 April 1738, only 21 years after the beginning of modern Freemasonry. "It is plain that the Popes from the later-modern era, Leo XIII included, strongly believed that many dangers threatening society were associated with the activities of Freemasonry.

The primary danger was the attempt to remove the Gospel of Christ from Western civilization by perverse means and doctrines as well as undermining (or overthrowing) the authority of the Catholic Church and civil governments."[85]

## FROM STILETTOS TO SUBTLETY

Letters between Freemasonic lodges that were obtained by the Church outlined the true aims and goals of the Freemasons. They were written in a time when assassinations in Italy were part of politics and labor as Italy was going through the pains of unification. Such murders at the hands of various Italian Freemasonic lodges such as the Carbonari and the Alta Vendita were far from uncommon. Monsignor George F. Dillon published several of these letters along with a series of his lectures in his book *The War of Antichrist With the Church and Christian Civilization*. One letter between members of the Alta Vendita, dated 9 August 1838, states:

*"To what purpose does it serve to kill a man? To strike fear into the timid and to keep audacious hearts far from us? Our predecessors ... did not understand their power. It is not the blood of an isolated man, or even of a traitor, that it is necessary to exercise it; it is upon the masses. Let us not individualize crime. In order to grow great, even to the proportions of patriotism and of hatred for the Church, it is necessary to generalize it.... Catholicism has no more fear of a well-sharpened stiletto than monarchies have, but these two bases of social order can fall by corruption. Let us then never cease to corrupt. Tertullian was right in saying, that the blood of martyrs was the seed of Christians. Let us, then, not make martyrs, but let us popularize vice among the multitudes. Let us cause them to draw it in by their five senses; to drink it in; to be saturated with it ... It is corruption en masse that we have undertaken: the corruption of the people by the clergy, and the corruption of the clergy by ourselves; the corruption which ought, one day to enable us to put the Church in her tomb. I have recently heard one of our friends, laughing in a philosophic manner at our projects, say to us: 'in order to destroy Catholicism it is necessary to commence*

by suppressing woman.' The words are true in a sense; but since we cannot suppress woman, let us corrupt her with the Church."[86]

In 1859, another letter that was circulated to members of several of the Freemasonic lodges in Italy was obtained by the Vatican. On the instruction of both Pope Pius IX and Pope Leo XIII, it was published first that same year by Jacques Crétineau-Joly in his book *L'Église romaine en face de la Révolution*, then later in English by Monsignor Dillon in 1885. The letter, entitled "The Permanent Instruction of the Alta Vendita," clearly spelled out their end goal:

"Our final end is that of Voltaire and of the French Revolution, the destruction for ever [sic] of Catholicism and even of the Christian idea which, if left standing on the ruins of Rome, would be the resuscitation of Christianity later on ... The Pope, whoever he may be, will never come to the secret societies. It is for the secret societies to come first to the Church.... The work which we have undertaken is not the work of a day, nor of a month, nor of a year. It may last many years, a century perhaps, but in our ranks the soldier dies and the fight continues.... Crush the enemy whoever he may be; crush the powerful by means of lies and calumnies; but especially crush him in the egg. It is to the youth we must go. It is that which we must seduce."[87]

In his commentary in 1885, Monsignor Dillon astutely notes the shift in tactics by the Freemasons away from assassinations and toward something more diabolical:

"They found out a more effective, though a far more infamous, way for attaining the dark mastery of the world. It was by the assassination not of bodies but of souls—by deliberate, systematic and persevering diffusion of immorality. The Alta Vendita, then, sat down calmly to consider the best means to accomplish this design. Satan and his fallen angels could devise no more efficacious methods than they found out. They resolved to spread impurity by every method used in the past by demons to tempt men to sin, to *make the practice of sin habitual, and to keep the unhappy victim in the state of sin to the end. They had, being living men, means to accomplish this purpose, which devils could not use without the aid of men.... So long as morality existed as a recognized virtue, the Revolution had no chance of permanent success; and so the men of the Alta Vendita resolved to bring back the world to a state of brutal licentiousness not only as bad as that of Paganism, but to a state at which even the morality of the Pagans would shudder. To do this they proceeded with caution. Their first attempt was to cause vice to lose its conventional horror, and to make it free from civil punishment.... Then literature was systematically rendered as immoral as possible, and diffused with a perseverance and labour worthy of a better cause. Railway stations, newspaper stands, book shops, and restaurants, were made to teem with infamous productions, while the same were scattered broadcast to the people over every land. The teaching of the Universities and of all the middle schools of the State, was not only to be rendered Atheistic and hostile to religion, but was actually framed to demoralize the unfortunate alumni at a season of life always but too prone to vice. Finally, besides the freest license for blasphemy and immorality, and the exhibition and diffusion of immoral pictures, paintings, and statuary, a last attempt was to be made upon the virtue of young females under the guise of educating them up to the standard of human progress. Therefore, middle and high-class schools were, regardless of expense, to be provided for female children, who should be, at any cost, taken far away from the protecting care of nuns. They were to be taught in schools directed by lay masters, and always exposed to such influences as would sap, if not destroy, their purity, and, as a sure consequence, their faith. These schools have since been the order of the day with Masonry all over the world.*"[88]

*"The first warning of the danger [of Freemasonry] was given by Clement XII in the year 1738, and his constitution was confirmed and renewed by Benedict XIV. Pius VII followed the same path; and Leo XII, by his apostolic constitution, Quo Graviora, put together the acts and decrees of former Pontiffs on this subject, and ratified and confirmed them forever. In the same sense spoke Pius VIII, Gregory XVI, and, many times over, Pius IX.*"[89]

What is important to note is that the Catholic Church has not changed her position on Freemasonry. In *Quaesitum Est*, issued by the Sacred Congregation for the Doctrine of the Faith on 26 November, 1983, it continues the warning against Freemasonry:

*"It has been asked whether there has been any change in the Church's decision in regard to Masonic associations since the new Code of Canon Law does not mention them expressly, unlike the previous code.... Therefore, the Church's negative judgment in regard to Masonic associations remains unchanged since their principles have always been considered irreconcilable with the doctrine of the Church and, therefore, membership in them remains forbidden. The faithful, who enroll in Masonic associations are in a state of grave sin and may not receive Holy Communion."* [90]

St. Maximilian Kolbe summed up Freemasonry thusly:

*"These men without God find themselves in a tragic situation. Such implacable hatred for the Church and the ambassadors of Christ on earth is not in the power of individual persons, but of a systematic activity stemming in the final analysis from Freemasonry. In particular, it aims to destroy the Catholic religion. Their deceits have been spread throughout the world, in different disguises. But with the same goal—religious indifference and weakening of moral forces, according to their basic principle—'We will conquer the Catholic Church not by argumentation, but rather with moral corruption.'"* [91]

By 1921, the decline of morality in society was so notable that Pope Benedict XV remarked in his Encyclical Letter *Sacra Propediem* that "there are two passions today dominant in the profound lawlessness of morals—an unlimited desire of riches and an insatiable thirst for pleasures." [92] He lamented that society's decline of morals was leading "it back to the ignominies of ancient paganism." Again, this was 1921 when skirt lengths in everyday fashion went just above the knee for the first time. By 1950, science fiction TV series *Space Patrol* hemlines had climbed to mid-thigh, and the show was targeted to children.

# VII. Building the Alternative

## BAITING THE TRAP

Have we turned around and regained the sense of sin? Hardly. We no longer perceive sin as sin, and instead have accelerated down that road, leaving behind the Church and morality for a new and more entertaining alternative. With the Freemasons, Satan set out to build an alternative to the Church, one that lured people out of their Domestic Churches with the empty promises of sins of the flesh. Now songs, movies, TV shows, books, and magazines glorify every imaginable sin against the 6th and 9th Commandments. The internet is awash in it. It is piped into our living rooms and we carry it in our pockets on our smartphones. We are indeed drinking it in, and are saturated with it. As "wardrobe malfunctions" scandalize Super Bowl halftime shows and pre-pubescent girls are lured into Victoria's Secret to buy "PINK" apparel, our children sing songs about sex, idolize the young stars who encourage promiscuity, and seek out a never-ending stream of obscene and perverse material while their parents prepare for divorce.

It is a safe assumption that most people who join the Freemasons probably don't know any of the backstory behind the organization. Perhaps they're looking for a group to join for social reasons. Maybe they join to network for business purposes. Perhaps they are looking for a group that can help them advance their political careers, get them out of a speeding ticket, or just something to belong to in order to get out of the house for a few hours now and then. Or maybe they join the Freemasons because they think it would be fun to join the Shriners and drive go-karts in parades. (In order to join Shriners International, you have to be a Mason. Shriners International was originally named the Ancient Arabic Order of Nobles of the Mystic Shrine as an appendant organization of the Freemasons.) They perceive the Masons as just a social club and nothing more.

Are Freemasons still actively pursuing goals to destroy Christianity in general and the Catholic Church in particular? That much isn't clear.

We do know that at one time, they did have those goals. We do know that the Catholic Church has not changed its opposition to Freemasonry, up to and including excommunication of any Catholic who joins a Freemasonic order or lodge. And we do know that Freemasons haven't changed their universalist/pantheistic interpretation of religion, which at its core is anti-Christian. "Catholics, as members [of the Freemasons], would be asked to put their membership of the lodge above their membership of the Church. The strict prohibition, in other words, was not for political purposes but for the care of souls. From the outset, the primary concern of the Church has been that Masonry suborns a Catholic's faith to that of the lodge, obliging them to place a fundamental secularist fraternity above communion with the Church."[93]

It is for these reasons that a long line of Popes condemned the Freemasons, and due to a growling list of secular assaults against the Church, Pope Leo XIII was simply continuing to sound the alarm. In 1884's *Humanum Genus*, "[h]e specifically referred to the aim of secularising [sic] the state and society.... He also decried the Masonic desire to remove the Church from any control in, or influence over, schools, hospitals, public charities, universities and any other body serving the public good. Also specifically highlighted was the Masonic push for the reimagining of marriage as a merely civil contract, the promotion of divorce, and support for the legalisation [sic] of abortion."[94]

### THE SENSE OF SIN IS LOST

The statue of Giordano Bruno was unveiled on 9 June 1889, to much fanfare. "[W]hile good Catholics celebrated Pentecost, Campo de' Fiori was festooned with flags bearing Masonic symbols. Fiery speeches were made by politicians, scholars and atheists about the importance of commemorating Bruno as one of the most original and oppressed freethinkers of his age.... [T]he Giordano Bruno Society subsequently opened an office a short walk from St. Peter's Square to taunt the Pope with its banners."[95] "Every year, on the anniversary of his execution, various groups of freethinkers—Masons, atheists, pantheists—gather at the monument, and a representative of Rome's mayoralty places a wreath at its feet."[96]

The choice of Giordano Bruno by the Freemasons as the subject of their statue was quite appropriate: Bruno's beliefs aligned so perfectly with their own. The "free thinking" heretic believed that even the demons would be reconciled to God, that there was no such thing as a sin too great, and that morality was all relative. What's more, the creation story and Original Sin and its effect on all of mankind were meaningless. As Cardinal Ratzinger (later Pope Benedict XVI) wrote, "At first sight it may seem strange to accuse him of suppressing faith in creation, since he was responsible for an emphatic rediscovery of the cosmos in its divinity. But it is precisely this reversion to a *divine* cosmos that brings about the recession of faith in creation."[97] With the cosmos divine in and of itself, rather than being a Divine creation, Giordano Bruno had plunged back into the dark and pagan waters of Greek and Roman gods and goddesses. This was exactly in line with Freemasonic thinking. As Cardinal Ratzinger continued, "In the final analysis, this is just the atheistic prelude to an increasingly prominent idea in the modern mind: the dependence implied by faith in creation is unacceptable. It is seen as the real barrier to human freedom, the basis of all other restrictions, the first thing needing to be eliminated if humankind is to be effectively liberated."[98] With that as a basis of thought, there didn't need to be a savior or a Church to believe in Him.

As Pope Leo XIII tells us:

*"without religion there is no true morality, either public or private. From the family, solidly based on its natural foundations, comes the life, the growth, and the energy of society. But without religion, and without morality, the domestic partnership has no stability, and the family bonds grow weak and*

*waste away.... It is religion which produces concord and affection between husband and wife, love and reverence between parents and their children; which makes the poor respect the property of others, and causes the rich to make a right use of their wealth. From this fidelity to duty, and this respect for the rights of others come the order, the tranquillity, and the peace, which form so large a part of the prosperity of a people and of a State. Take away religion, and with it all these immensely precious benefits would disappear from society."* [99]

Satan stands opposed to all of this. He wants no affection between husband and wife. He wants no love or reverence between parents and their children. He doesn't want the poor to respect the property of others, nor does he want the rich to make the right use of their wealth. He wants no order, no tranquility, and no peace. To accomplish this, Satan uses the Freemasons to destroy religion by destroying morality, replacing the Church with an amoral alternative: the sins of vice, and in particular, sins of the flesh, all targeted at children just as Our Lady of Good Success told Sister Marianna would come to pass. The temples of sin built by the Freemasons have been drawing people out of the Domestic Church in droves. The ivy of misperception continues to grow and do damage, and there are fewer and fewer people left inside to hold up the walls and try to repair the damage.

And Satan has schemes to get those people to leave too.

# VIII. A Knock at the Door

"Now the snake was the most cunning of all
the wild animals that the Lord God had made."

GENESIS 3:1

# VIII. A Knock at the Door

IN 1846, Pope Pius IX penned an encyclical entitled *Qui Pluribus*, (On Faith And Religion.) In it, he warned of dangers to come against the Church and her people and exhorted those who read it to "keep the night-watches over the flock entrusted to your care with the greatest possible eagerness, wakefulness and effort." He minced no words as he wrote of "the most dark designs of men in the clothing of sheep, while inwardly ravening wolves. They humbly recommend themselves by means of a feigned and deceitful appearance of a purer piety, a stricter virtue and discipline; after taking their captives gently, they mildly bind them, and then kill them in secret. They make men fly in terror from all practice of religion, and they cut down and dismember the sheep of the Lord. To this end, finally—to omit other dangers which are too well known to you—tends the widespread disgusting infection from books and pamphlets which teach the lessons of sinning. These works, well-written and filled with deceit and cunning, are scattered at immense cost through every region for the destruction of the Christian people. They spread pestilential doctrines everywhere and deprave the minds especially of the imprudent, occasioning great losses for religion."[100]

Thirty-eight years later, in 1884—the same year that Pope Leo XIII wrote *Humanum Genus* to address Freemasonry—a British playwright by the name of George Bernard Shaw became one of the founding members of a British socialist group called the Fabian Society. They took their name from the Roman general Fabius Maximus, who beat his enemies by waiting them out instead of direct confrontation. The Society was started as a discussion club,[101] but with the arrival of Shaw, it quickly gained momentum and purpose. "Quite simply, they wanted to change the world through a species of propaganda termed 'education,' which would lead to political action."[102] Shaw was a fan of the philosophies of Karl Marx and was friends with his daughter Eleanor Marx. He traveled, wrote, lectured, and along with other members of the Society, published pamphlets or "tracts" in both

England and the United States in order to advance their philosophies and agenda. Of note, the Fabian Society's coat of arms, prominently displayed in a stained glass window at the Fabian-born London School of Economics, is a wolf in sheep's clothing,

The Fabian Society can be seen as a "Socialism incubator," giving money and support to upstarts and offshoots. They helped set up countless clubs, societies, and associations, both in England and in the United States, to spread their ideas. These groups were set up with their own people and their well-groomed followers guiding every action. They had innocent-sounding names like the Nationalist Club, the Oxford Social Club, and the Boston Bellamy Club. One notable group in England, the Christian Book Club, was run by the same publisher as the Left Book Club, and "[t]he first book this Club recommended for Christian readers was *Soviet Socialism, A New Civilisation* [sic], by [Fabian Society co-founders] Sidney and Beatrice Webb—the same work which had been prepared with the aid of the Soviet Secret Police and which announced the Soviets' fabled policy of tolerance towards religion. Members of the so-called Christian Book Club were also privileged to purchase virtually the whole list of the Left Book Club selections at the reduced prices." [103]

In his 1890 tract "What Socialism Is," Shaw says:

*"Poverty and riches together mean the perversion of our capital and industry to the production of frippery and luxury whilst the nation is rotting for want of good food, thorough instruction, and wholesome clothes and dwellings for the masses. What we want in order to make true progress is more bakers, more schoolmasters, more wool-weavers and tailors, and more builders; what we get instead is more footmen, more gamekeepers, more jockeys, and more prostitutes.... Socialism means equal rights and opportunities for all."* [104]

## CHRISTIAN SOCIALISM

"Early in the game, Shaw confided to the German Socialist, Eduard Bernstein, that he wanted the Fabians to be 'the Jesuits of Socialism.'"[105] And indeed, Shaw and the Fabian Society gathered as many respectable people in the religious life as they could. They primarily recruited from various Protestant denominations men like Reverend Stewart Headlam, Reverend William Morris, Reverend Percy Dearmer, and Reverend Thomas Hancock.[106] As Sister Mary Margaret McCarran noted, "It was Fabian practice to evade responsibility on the part of the Society by notice that the Fabian Tracts represented their author's views, and not official views of the Society, but nothing in their history indicates they could have published a Catholic response on the birth control question."[107] "For the most part its spokesmen prudently avoided outraging the beliefs of religious-minded persons, while soliciting their support for Socialist candidates and projects. The Christian Book Club was a unique but significant venture for which the Society, as usual, disclaimed any official responsibility."[108]

In this regard, the Fabian Society excelled at shrugging its shoulders while they sowed the seeds of Socialism. They published several tracts that all preached the twisted "social gospel" known as Christian Socialism. From 1892 onward, they published tracts like Reverend John Clifford's "Socialism and the Teaching of Christ," Reverend Dearmer's "Socialism and Christianity," and Reverend Headlam's "Christian Socialism," which were all geared to distort people's perceptions of the truth about Christ. They all used their perceived clerical authority to convince readers that all the miracles of Christ were, in fact, "distinctly secular, socialist works: works for health against disease, works restoring beauty and harmony and pleasure where there had been ugliness and discord and misery; works taking care to see that the people were properly fed."[109]

This is in direct opposition to the words of Jesus Christ Himself. Let us look at the story of the man blind from birth. Jews believed that such a condition was due to sin, with some Jews believing it was sin inherited from the parents, while other Jews believed it was sin the man had committed in a previous life. To settle the dispute, "His disciples asked him, 'Rabbi, who sinned, this man or his parents, that he was born blind?' Jesus answered, 'Neither he nor his parents sinned; it is so that the works of God might be made visible through him.'"[110] Jesus performed miracles so that people would see the works of God, and by performing miracles, Jesus "revealed his glory" (John 2:11). But now, taking advantage of what was set in motion by Martin Luther 300 years prior, everyone was free to use his own perception to determine for himself what the Bible meant. In turn, that flexibility gave these reverends the license to interpret the word of God however they wanted, with little to no oversight regarding errant or heretical beliefs. Jesus said, "I came into this world for judgment, so that those who do not see might see, and those who do see might become blind,"[111] yet the Christian Socialists taught that He was sent to give us an example for how to enact social reform. They claimed that Jesus taught "just the very thing that the Socialists teach. We shall be saved or condemned according to our acts of social service, saying nothing about church-going, or conversion, or orthodoxy...."[112]

The Catholic Church has historically stood in opposition to the false teachings of Socialism. Pope Pius IX spoke out against Socialism in his encyclical *Nostis et Nobiscum* in 1849, saying it contained "wicked theories" and "perverted teachings."[113] Pope Leo XIII devoted the entire 1878 encyclical *Quod Apostolici Muneris* to Socialism, saying of Socialists that, "[t]hey refuse obedience to the higher powers, to whom, according to the admonition of the Apostle, every soul ought to be subject, and who derive the right of governing from God; and they proclaim the absolute equality of all men in rights and duties. They debase the natural union of man and woman, which is held sacred even among barbarous peoples; and its bond, by which the family is chiefly held together, they weaken, or even deliver up to lust.... [T]he boldness of these bad men, which day by day more and more threatens civil society with destruction, and strikes the souls of all with anxiety and fear, finds its cause and origin in those poisonous doctrines which, spread abroad in former times among the people, like evil seed bore in due time such fatal fruit."

Understanding the importance of marriage and the danger Socialism posed to it, *Quod Apostolici Muneris* continued:

*"[T]he foundation of this society rests first of all in the indissoluble union of man and wife according to the necessity of natural law, and is completed in the mutual rights and duties of parents and children, masters and servants. You know also that the doctrines of socialism strive almost completely to dissolve this union; since, that stability which is imparted to it by religious wedlock being lost, it follows that the power of the father over his own children, and the duties of the children toward their parents, must be greatly weakened. But the Church, on the contrary, teaches that 'marriage, honorable in all,' which God himself instituted in the very beginning of the world, and made indissoluble for the propagation and preservation of the human species, has become still more binding and more holy through Christ, who raised it to the dignity of a sacrament, and chose to use it as the figure of His own union with the Church."* [114]

### THE SOCIAL GOSPEL

Despite these warnings, the lies of the "social gospel" wormed their way into the Catholic Church as well. One notable example, which illustrates how Fabian Socialism grows and spreads while maintaining respectability and deniability, is Monsignor John Ryan. While attending St. Paul Seminary in 1894, Msgr. Ryan read Pope Leo XIII's encyclical *Rerum Novarum* on the rights of capital and labor. The encyclical was very balanced and clearly outlined the duties and rights of both the worker and the employer, and the role that Church and State were to play in this relationship. On multiple occasions, the encyclical stated that the law should favor ownership of property, that it was against natural law and justice to deprive someone of the property he had worked for, and that the government's responsibility was to act as the protector of the rights of both the employer and the laborer. Monsignor Ryan seemed to latch on to phrases such as "wage-earners, since they mostly belong in the mass of the needy, should be specially cared for and protected by the government," and ignored phrases such as "Let the working man and the employer make free agreements, and in particular let them agree freely as to the wages."

Monsignor Ryan went on to write *A Living Wage* in 1906, which "professes, nay, urges, a definite and considerable measure of industrial justice"[115] and calls for the government to institute a minimum wage. Of note, Msgr. Ryan credits Fabian Socialist John Hobson and co-founders of the Fabian Society Sidney and Beatrice Webb in the preface of this book. In 1919, after the end of World War I, he unveiled a draft of a postwar "social reconstruction" plan. In it, he praised the "four pillars" of a similar plan, "Labour and the New Social Order," written by Sidney Webb for the British Labour Party. Rose L. Martin explains his approach, saying, "True to Catholic orthodoxy, 'complete Socialism' must be rejected; but not the bulk of the ill-begotten Fabian 'reform' program. Illogically, Father Ryan praised the means while rejecting the end. Although his views certainly cannot be regarded as typical of the Catholic leaders of his day, he left disciples behind him and founded a school of thought which has since come to be accepted unquestioningly by many otherwise devout Catholic teachers and students of the social sciences."[116] Monsignor Ryan went on to help Franklin D. Roosevelt get elected, and then he helped provide support and guidance in crafting the New Deal.

While Msgr. Ryan stayed loyal to Catholic teaching and orthodoxy in all matters, it is illustrative to note how subtle the Fabian Socialist infiltration is, how it works, and how it spreads. Here is, again, an intelligent man and a respectable man. He was revered and influential. And with a slight twisting here and a little over-emphasis there, he was led to unwittingly assist the Socialists in their goals. While publicly rejecting Socialism in order to maintain his Catholic orthodoxy, he was approving of government policies that were totally Socialist in both their origin and in their final objective. Under his guidance, Catholics could in turn vote for such politicians and embrace such policies with a clear conscience, believing that they were in line with Catholic teaching. Make no mistake, their goals sound noble enough on the surface, which is why people listen and rally around the ideas proposed by the Fabian Socialists in the first place. But when you dig deeper and discover the truth, you find that all of their goals are pointing toward an upheaval of society and a restructuring of the social order, including the upheaval and restructuring of the family. The political and economic pieces are simply all supporting parts of the same plan.

## GOING DOOR-TO-DOOR

Let's imagine there's a knock on your door, and when you answer it, there's a traveling salesman. He says, "Here is this kitchen appliance I want to sell you. It's awesome. Amazing. A little expensive, but it will change your life! If you plug it in and turn it on, it will explode and destroy your house with 100% certainty." You'd probably laugh and wonder what kind of crazy person this was, and you'd shut the door and get back to what you were doing. You wouldn't buy such a crazy appliance, not in a million years. The next day, another knock. Another traveling salesman. He's selling replacement filters for this kitchen appliance ... oh, you don't have one? That's too bad. Before he goes, would you like to see a picture of his family? So even though you don't need it, you buy a package of filters from him for the appliance you don't own. He has a family to support and all. Then the next day, another traveling salesman knocks, and you buy another part for the appliance you don't own or even want because you feel sorry for him too. One after another traveling salesman comes to your door, and because you feel sorry for each of them, you buy whatever they're selling, even though you don't have the kitchen appliance that uses the parts they're selling.

Then one hot day, a man comes along asking if you need service for this kitchen appliance you don't own or even want. You tell him you don't own one. He says, okay, then asks if he could trouble you for a glass of water, it being so hot outside and all. You feel sorry for him and let him in. He looks around and sees all the boxes for all the parts. "You don't own one? Well, why do you have all the parts?" You explain you bought them because you felt sorry for the traveling salesmen who were selling them. He laughs and says, "Well, friend, you have every part needed to make that appliance. I could put it together for you in no time at all. I have a family to feed too, you know. Just because I put it together doesn't mean you have to *use* it." So, feeling sorry for the man, you pay him to assemble the appliance. He starts putting it together, and as soon as the last piece is in place, it starts to shake and smoke and bursts into flames. In moments, your entire kitchen is engulfed in flames. Everyone runs out of the house, the fire department comes and puts out the fire, and you stand there, looking at the smoking, water-logged remains of your house. "What did you do?!" you exclaim. "My house is ruined!"

Just then, the first salesman walks up, the one who wanted to sell you the whole appliance. "Told ya it would change your life!" he says with a smile, and walks off.

You start to yell at the serviceman, the one who put it all together. "You said I didn't have to use it! I never wanted to use it! I didn't even want it! I just felt sorry for you! I felt sorry for all of you! I never wanted to destroy my house! *Why did you turn it on?!*"

He shrugs. "Once it's all together, it just runs. You don't have to plug it in. There is no 'on' switch. And you can't shut it off." And he walks away.

Socialism comes to you like a long parade of traveling salesmen. Each part of it, on its own, sounds good. Each part of the Socialism machine appeals to your emotions, and is sold by people whom you perceive you can trust, who don't seem like they would support the evils of Socialism. You perceive that you can trust your priest when he talks about the great good that will come from government programs and the higher taxes to pay for them. You perceive that you can trust your doctor when he talks to you about the importance of genetic screening of your unborn child. You perceive that you can trust a scientific study that comes out warning of the strain overpopulation is putting on global resources. You perceive that a politician who runs on a platform of helping working mothers by expanding government-run childcare services is doing a good service for the community. Each of these people unknowingly advances the platform of Socialism one step at a time by appealing to our perceptions. Income redistribution, abortion and eugenics, palliative care and euthanasia, destruction of the family ... Socialism. If one of these words, say, for example, "eugenics," acquires a bad connotation for some reason, they simply re-package the message with new words. They simply replace "eugenics" with words like "genetic screening" and continue to promote the lie. "Thus, gradual and penetrating Socialism came to be accepted as mere reformism.... One no longer even needed to read Marx and Engels in order to advance their programs."[117]

## WALKING AWAY

The Socialist messages against God and religion are as subtle as the serpent's asking Eve, "Did God really say, 'You shall not eat from any of the trees in the garden'?" Those left in the Domestic Church, the ones trying to hold up the walls after others have been lured away by vice, are left looking at a building that doesn't seem worth saving. "It's too much trouble, isn't it?" the serpent says. "Wouldn't it be easier to just ... leave? Find a new church? Heck, who needs churches anyway. They're so much trouble. You don't need them. You don't have time. By the way, have you seen the new government-run services that will make your life easier?"

And one by one, people leave their Domestic Churches. When one spouse is lured out by sin or vice, the other grows weary of trying to hold it up on his own. The walls are weakened by the ivy of misperception and the inside is burned out by the exploding appliance they never wanted. Looking around, it's all too easy to just walk away. Sometimes this happens in a literal sense, when spouses separate or divorce. Sometimes, it's figurative, when spouses remain married but drift so far apart they lead completely separate lives. Either way, Satan's plan for people to abandon their Domestic Churches is working. Every day there are fewer and fewer Domestic Churches to hold up Christ's Church. Resistance to Satan is growing weaker.

All that's left is to knock down what remains by force.

# IX. Sledgehammers and Sickles

"They charge the city, they run upon the wall,
they climb into the houses; Through the windows
they enter like thieves. Before them the earth trembles;
the heavens shake; Sun and moon are darkened,
and the stars withhold their brightness."

Joel 2:9-10

# IX. Sledgehammers and Sickles

IN ADDITION to the founding of the Fabian Society and the writing of *Humanum Genus* against Freemasonry, one other notable event happened in 1884: Friedrich Engels, noted associate of Karl Marx, published *The Origin of the Family, Private Property, and the State*. This work advanced the views of Marx and Engels against the nature of marriage and family and attacked traditional gender roles. "While Marx once alluded to a higher form of the family in communist society, he and Engels usually wrote about the destruction, dissolution, and abolition of the family. The relationships they envisaged for communist society would have little or no resemblance to the family as it existed in nineteenth-century Europe or indeed anywhere else. Thus it is certainly appropriate to define their position as the abolition of the family."[118]

Engels created the notion that women in a traditional family are slaves of their husbands, and claimed that monogamy was based on economic rather than natural conditions. Engels' work advocated for free and easy divorce; eliminating gender-specific roles in the family; turning housework into an industry and removing the notion of the woman as the housekeeper; turning childcare over to the community; eliminating the stigma of illegitimate pregnancies; making the definition of marriage flexible; and removing restraint on sexual activity of all forms, among other things. After publishing *The Origin of the Family, Private Property, and the State*, Engels traveled to the United States in 1884 to spread his ideas, but he was rejected by working-class Americans because "Engels' godless views on religion and marriage, as expressed in his *Origin of the Family*, were widely publicized."[119]

As we saw the slow building of William of Ockham's ideas into the atheistic ideas of The Age of Reason, the works of Marx and Engels were similarly seeds of Communism. Vladimir Lenin wrote: "Engels was the finest scholar and teacher of the modern proletariat in the whole civilized world.... In their scientific works, Marx and Engels were the first to explain that socialism is not the invention of dreamers, but the final aim and necessary result of the development of the productive forces in modern society." [120]

Make no mistake: Communism is more than just an economic and political movement. At its roots it is a social movement. It is, then, necessarily a movement based in the destruction of the family. As early as 1846, the Church identified the dangers of this growing philosophy in Pope Pius IX's Papal Encyclical *Qui Pluribus:* "To this goal also tends the unspeakable doctrine of Communism, as it is called, a doctrine most opposed to the very natural law. For if this doctrine were accepted, the complete destruction of everyone's laws, government, property, and even of human society itself would follow." [121]

In 1891, the Church's opposition to Marx and Engels' beliefs on the family were made even clearer by Pope Leo XIII in his Papal Encyclical *Rerum Novarum*, stating,

*"The contention, then, that the civil government should at its option intrude into and exercise intimate control over the family and the household is a great and pernicious error.... And for the very reason that 'the child belongs to the father' it is, as St. Thomas Aquinas says, 'before it attains the use of free will, under the power and the charge of its parents.' The socialists, therefore, in setting aside the parent and setting up a State supervision, act against natural justice, and destroy the structure of the home."* [122]

We know that Satan's goal is to take everything God has created and turn it upside down. Looking at the goals of Communism we see that its goal is to take everything in modern society, and turn it upside down. "Karl Marx is the natural father of all modern Social Democracy, not excluding those groups which for reasons of propriety choose to deny or dissemble the relationship. As the writings of Marx disclose, that herald of 'the new social order' hated all religions with impartial fervor. Marx visualized the Class War—since his time a basic concept in both Socialist and Communist philosophy—as being essentially an inverted crusade against the Deity whose existence he denied. *Non serviam* ('I will not serve'), the phrase of Lucifer before the Fall, is innate in the dogmas of Marx."[123]

The work of Engels and Marx found fertile ground when Lenin met a young revolutionary named Josef Stalin. Josef was raised by his devout Russian Orthodox Christian mother, and an abusive alcoholic father who once beat Josef so badly that his elbow suffered an injury that lasted him the rest of his life. The desires of his parents for him to become a priest faded as he dropped out of seminary. He then joined the Social Democratic Labor Party and declared himself to be an atheist. He is reported to have said, "You know, they are fooling us, there is no God... all this talk about God is sheer nonsense."[124] The Bolshevik revolution of 1917 propelled Stalin—and his godless agenda—into power.

### COMMUNISM: SATAN'S ENDGAME

Religion in general and Christianity, in particular, are so repugnant to Communists that they have been universally attacked in every Communist nation. "'The Russian people were the first to suffer under an atheistic and godless government,' said the Rev. Victor Potapov, head pastor of the Russian Orthodox Cathedral of St. John the Baptist in Northwest."[125] According to information gathered by *The Tablet*, in the aftermath of the Bolshevik Revolution of 1917, there were 106,000 Russian Orthodox clergy shot during the Great Purge. During that same period, 422 Catholic priests were executed or tortured to death. The Communist regime also executed 962 monks, nuns, and laypeople. All but two Catholic Churches were seized by the government and repurposed for "the common good."[126] Christians in the Soviet Union after World War II were compulsively sent to mental hospitals or forcibly deprived of their parental rights.[127] To remove any doubt that Satan influenced the Communist movement, it bears mentioning that Soviet Russia developed the League of Militant Atheists in 1925 to advance the policies and views of the Communist Party of the Soviet Union.[128] Its goal was the removal of God and religion from the lives of everyone in the Soviet Union, because godlessness was determined to be essential to the advancement of Communism.

Pope Pius XI wrote a Papal Encyclical discussing the evils of Communism named *Divini Redemptoris,* which was published on 19 March 1937. In it, he stated:

*"Refusing to human life any sacred or spiritual character, such a doctrine logically makes of marriage and the family a purely artificial and civil institution, the outcome of a specific economic system. There exists no matrimonial bond of a juridico-moral nature that is not subject to the whim of the individual or of the collectivity. Naturally, therefore, the notion of an indissoluble marriage-tie is scouted. Communism is particularly characterized by the rejection of any link that binds woman to the family and the home, and her emancipation is proclaimed as a basic principle. She is withdrawn from the family and the care of her children, to be thrust instead into public life and collective production under the same conditions as man. The care of home and children then devolves upon the collectivity. Finally, the right of education is denied to parents, for it is conceived as the exclusive prerogative of the community, in whose name and by whose mandate alone parents may exercise this right."* [129]

The Pope's words may be a bit fancy and, in a way, sugar-coated Communism's views on marriage and the family. Vladimir Lenin, interviewed by radical activist Clara Zetkin, was much more straightforward and, dare we say, blunt:

*"The decay, the corruption, the filth of bourgeois marriage, with its difficult divorce, its freedom for the man, its enslavement for the woman, the repulsive hypocrisy of sexual morality and relations fill the most active minded and best people with deep disgust.... The constraint of bourgeois marriage and the family laws of bourgeois states accentuate these evils and*

*conflicts. It is the force of 'holy property'. It sanctifies venality, degradation, filth.... Sex and marriage forms, in their bourgeois sense, are unsatisfactory. A revolution in sex and marriage is approaching, corresponding to the proletarian revolution.... Nothing could be more false than to preach monkish asceticism and the sanctity of dirty bourgeois morality to the youth."* [130]

Within months after World War II ended, Communism began spreading quickly throughout Europe and Asia. Take, for example, Albania. In November 1944, Albanian resistance forces—who were aided by the Soviet Union—drove the Nazis out of the country. Within a year, the Communist Democratic Front of Albania gained power, and in December 1945, the persecution of Christians in general and Catholics, in particular, began under dictator Enver Hoxha. Hoxha perceived the Catholic Church as a foreign power that not only would challenge his regime but also a source of alternate loyalty for the people. As such, his war on the Church began in earnest.

The sham trials began almost immediately, and public executions started taking place in March of 1946. "Priests were drowned in latrines, shot, imprisoned merely for the possession of religious items, and some, including a young nun, Maria Tuci, were tied in bags with wild animals." [131] And this was just the beginning. Religious buildings that weren't destroyed were re-purposed for secular uses. For example, the Catholic Cathedral in Shkodra was turned into a gymnasium. Catholic priest Shtjefen Kurti spent 20 years in jail, then was monitored by over a dozen government agents. At the age of 72, he was caught performing Baptisms in secret and was re-arrested. They charged him with sabotage, espionage, and secretly conducting religious ceremonies and executed him. Father Ernest Simoni Troshani was arrested, tortured, and sentenced to 25 years in prison doing hard labor in Albanian mines. [132]

Author Robert Royal, in his article for the Catholic Education Resource Center entitled "Albania: The First Atheist State," recounts the stories of martyrdom of numerous laity, priests, bishops, and archbishops in Hoxha's Albania. He also quotes from the journal of Jan Gardin, a Jesuit survivor of the Communist prison camps:

*"Most of them were beaten on their bare feet with wooden clubs; the fleshy part of the legs and buttocks were cut open, rock salt inserted beneath the skin, and then sewn up again; their feet, placed in boiling water until the flesh fell off, were then rubbed with salt; their Achilles tendons were pierced with hot wires. Some were hung by their arms for three days without food; put in ice and icy water until nearly frozen; had electrical wires placed in their ears, nose, mouth, genitals, and anus; burning pine needles placed under fingernails; forced to eat a kilo of salt and having water withheld for 24 hours; boiled eggs put in their armpits; teeth pulled without anesthetic; tied behind vans and dragged; left in solitary confinement without food or water until almost dead; forced to drink their own urine and eat their own excrement; put in pits of excrement up to their necks; put on a bed of nails and covered with heavy material; put in nail-studded cages which were then rotated rapidly."* [133]

Propaganda movies and news stories turned citizen against citizen. Worse still, indoctrination of children at the public schools turned children against their own parents. Homes were routinely bugged with listening devices, and the Sigurimi—the Albanian secret police— interrogated people frequently.[134]

Unsurprisingly, the Catholic Church found Communism so diabolically evil that a 1949 decree stated that any Catholic who supported Communism in any way, including voting for or supporting any Communist political official, was automatically excommunicated from the Catholic Church.[135]

On the other side of the continent, Christians met a similar fate at the hands of the Chinese Communists. "The Chinese Communist Party was aggressively atheistic and targeted all religions in the country for destruction. The Catholic Church, with its many missionaries from America and Europe and its ties to Rome and the entire universal Church, gave the communists the ammunition they wanted to depict Catholics as counterrevolutionaries, spies and the tools of foreign imperialists."[136] Throughout the 1950s, thousands of Christians were arrested, imprisoned, tortured, and murdered by the Chinese Communists. "By 1960, every Catholic institution and every Catholic church in Shanghai had been expropriated by the communists. Catholics—clergy, religious and laity—who would not renounce their allegiance to the Pope were imprisoned or sent to labor camps."[137]

Back in Albania, the persecution of religion was reaching a fever pitch. Inspired by China's Cultural Revolution, on 6 February 1967, Enver Hoxha delivered a speech that began the Communist's official battle against religious ideology by declaring a "Cultural and Ideological Revolution," proudly proclaiming Albania as the first officially atheistic country. Shortly thereafter, it was a common sight to see trucks filled with people who were sent to camps to ensure their loyalty by showing them what would befall them if they kept their faith. Nine years later, the Albanian constitution boldly stated: "The state recognizes no religion and supports and develops atheistic propaganda to engage people in the materialistic scientific worldview," and explicitly forbid the establishment of any religion. By 1982, all religious-named cities were renamed, and the Albanian government made people's religious-based first names illegal. In the same year, the Albanian government published an official *Dictionary of People's Names* that contained approximately 3,000 approved secular names.

Communism is the complete inversion of God's creation for society. Not a single one of the Ten Commandments is protected under Communism. It is society that is rooted in Satan's rebellious cry,

"I will not serve!" Yet today, in every nation around the world, the cries for more Socialism and Communism grow louder every day.

Getting to this point did not happen overnight. The ivy of misperception of the Bolshevik Revolution didn't immediately appear to pose a problem in November of 1917. But sadly, it has been allowed to grow virtually unimpeded for over a century, its damage silently impacting every area of our lives. Domestic Churches are falling, one after the other. Churches are being emptied, one after the other. And souls are being lost for all eternity.

If only we would have listened to our Mother.

# X. Our Lady of Fatima

"A great sign appeared in the sky,
a woman clothed with the sun, with the moon
under her feet, and on her head a crown of twelve stars."

APOCALYPSE 12:1

THE anti-religious fervor started by Pombal after the earthquake and flood of Lisbon was stirred up again during the drafting of the constitution of the First Portuguese Republic in 1910. "Catholic churches and schools were seized by the government, and the wearing of clerics in public, the ringing of church bells, and the celebrating of popular religious festivals were banned. Between 1911–1916, nearly 2,000 priests, monks and nuns were killed by anti-Christian groups."[138] Portugal was lauded by Lenin as the most atheistic nation in the world.

Then on 13 May 1917, with World War I still raging, something miraculous happened.

Three illiterate shepherd children, Lucia dos Santos and her cousins Francisco and Jacinta Marto, were in a field in the Cova da Iria, near Fatima, Portugal. They were tending their sheep when they saw an apparition of the Blessed Virgin Mary appear resting on top of an oak tree. She told the children that she would return there on the thirteenth of each month for the next five months and that they were to learn to read and write, to pray the Rosary each day, and to offer sacrifices for the conversion of sinners. As word of the apparition spread, people began gathering at Fatima on the thirteenth of the month, and a makeshift shrine was constructed at the Cova da Iria.

About fifty people came on 13 June 1917. All three children could see Mary, but only Lucia and Jacinta could hear Mary speak. The others who gathered could not see Mary, but they saw and heard other things: tree branches bending as if someone was sitting on them, a little cloud rising from the Cova da Iria, a faint murmur of someone speaking.

In July the number of onlookers grew to 5,000. During this apparition, Mary gave the children a secret in three parts and promised to perform a miracle on 13 October to prove to everyone that the apparitions were real and that the children were to be believed. In the first part of the secret, after telling the children to make sacrifices for sinners, Mary showed them a vision of Hell. Lucia recounted in her memoirs:

*"As Our Lady spoke these last words, she opened her hands once more as she had done during the previous two months. The rays of light seemed to penetrate the earth, and we saw as it were a sea of fire. Plunged in this fire were demons and souls in human form, like transparent burning embers, all blackened or burnished bronze, floating about in the conflagration, now raised into the air by the flames that issued from within themselves, together with great clouds of smoke now falling back on every side like sparks in huge fires, without weight or equilibrium, amid shrieks and groans of pain and despair, which horrified us and made us tremble with fear. (It must have been this sight which caused me to cry out, as people say they heard me.) The demons could be distinguished by their terrifying and repellent likeness to frightful and unknown animals, black and transparent like burning coals. Terrified and as if to plead for succor, we looked up at Our lady, who said to us, so kindly and so sadly: 'You have seen Hell where the souls of poor sinners go.'"*[139]

She told the children not to reveal the secret until they had been told by her to do so. The Masonic newspaper in Lisbon, *O Seculo*, ridiculed the apparitions, the seers, and those who went to the Cova da Iria. The paper contained mocking cartoons and an article titled, "A Celestial Embassy ... Financial Speculation?" that accused the townsfolk of concocting the story for tourism purposes, hoping to find a spring of mineral water so that they could become a pilgrimage destination like Lourdes, France.[140]

On the morning of 13 August, before the next apparition, mayor Arthur Santos—a member of the Masonic Lodge of Leiria—abducted the three children and imprisoned them. He believed that if the children were not present at the Cova, nothing would happen, and this ridiculous mess would be over. He ruthlessly interrogated the children, threatening to boil them in oil if they didn't reveal the secret to him or else confess that they were lying. The children remained faithful to Mary's instructions not to reveal the secret, even unto the threat of death. In the meantime, the crowds had swelled to around 20,000 people. At the appointed hour, eyewitnesses reported that there was a flash of lightning, rolling thunder, and "a blue and white cloud descending and then shortly afterwards rising and disappearing."[141] Other eyewitnesses reported, "While looking around us, we observed a strange thing, which we had already seen the previous time, and which we were going to see again in the future. The faces of the people had all the colors of the rainbow: pink, red, blue ... The trees did not appear to have branches and leaves but only flowers; everything seemed laden with flowers, and every leaf appeared to be a flower. The ground was covered with squares of different colors. Clothes were also of every color of the rainbow."[142] Since the children weren't at the Cova da Iria on the 13th, Mary came to the children on 19 August, telling them, "I want you to continue going to the Cova da Iria on the 13th, that you continue praying the Rosary every day. On the last month, I will perform a miracle so that all may believe."[143]

"The Masonic Lodge at Santarem, a neighboring town to Fatima, became the rallying point to atheistic opposition to Our Lady of Fatima. In September 1917, men from Santarem joined up with men from Vila Nova de Ourém and marched to the site of the apparitions at the Cova da Iria. They proceeded to attack the make-shift shrine with axes."[144] Despite this, the September apparition drew approximately 30,000 people, and Mary told the children again that in October she would perform a miracle so that all would believe.

On 13 October 1917, Fatima was wet and rainy, the ground muddy and people's clothes soaked. Eyewitness reports say it was completely overcast and raining heavily.[145] Dominic Reis, who had traveled 100 miles to Fatima, said, "There was a good three inches of water where I stood and mud on the ground. I was soaking wet. Then around noon time, the sun started breaking through the clouds and we could see the sun. Now it was raining just like you open a faucet in your house."[146] Estimates of the crowd averaged about 70,000, a mix of believers and skeptics. And then the rain stopped, the clouds disappeared, and Mary arrived. Before the miracle, she took on "a more sorrowful air" and told Lucia, "Do not offend the Lord Our God anymore, for He is already too much offended!" And then the Miracle of the Sun began.

Eyewitness reports say the sun dimmed, so you could look at it without shielding your eyes, then it "shook and trembled; it seemed like a wheel of fire." "The sun turned like a fire wheel, taking on all the colors of the rainbow." "Everything assumed those same colors: our faces, our clothes, the earth itself." Then: "We suddenly heard a clamor, like a cry of anguish of that entire crowd. The sun, in fact, keeping its rapid movement of rotation, seemed to free itself from the firmament and, blood-red, to plunge towards the earth, threatening to crush us with its fiery mass. Those were some terrifying seconds."

There were also cases of instantaneous conversions: "There was an unbeliever there who had spent the morning mocking the simpletons who had gone off to Fatima just to see an ordinary girl. He now seemed paralyzed, his eyes fixed on the sun. He began to tremble from head to foot, and lifting up his arms, fell on his knees in the mud, crying out to God." People prayed for mercy, crying out in repentance for their sins. Dominic Reis continued, "Everyone was hollering out. We were all so afraid. Some started to confess their sins openly before everyone. Even my mother grabbed me to herself and started to cry, saying... 'Dominic, this is the end of the world.'"[147] Then the sun stopped and rose back to the sky and everyone noticed that everything—their clothes, the ground, truly everything—was dry. This event lasted for ten minutes, and was seen by people in villages some miles away.[148]

Avelino de Almeida, the editor-in-chief of *O Seculo* who was on hand to personally debunk the apparitions, reported, "And then we witnessed a unique spectacle, an incredible spectacle, unbelievable if you did not witness it. From above the road we see the immense crowd turn towards the sun, which appeared at its zenith, clear of the clouds. It looked like a plate of dull silver, and it was possible to stare at it without the least discomfort. It did not burn the eyes. It did not blind." At a later date, he wrote in a letter:

*"when I no longer imagined that I was seeing anything more impressive than that noisy but peaceful multitude animated by the same obsessive idea and moved by the same powerful yearning, what did I see on that occasion in the shrubland of Fatima that was truly extraordinary? I saw the rain cease to fall at the predicted time; I saw the dense mass of clouds break up and the Sun—a disc of opaque silver—appear at full zenith and begin a violent and convulsive dance, which a great number of people imagined to be a serpentine dance, so beautiful and resplendent were the colors successively adorning the solar surface. Miracle, as the people shouted; natural phenomenon, as the wise say? I don't profess to know right now, but only to affirm to you what I saw... The rest is with Science and with the Church... (emphasis in original)."* [149]

After careful investigation, the Catholic Church declared the event approved as "worthy of belief" in 1930.

Over the course of the apparitions, Mary revealed to the children a vision of Hell; the end of World War I and, if her instructions were not followed, the coming of World War II; and that "Russia will spread its errors throughout the world." Obviously, her instructions were not followed, and her prophecies came true. Two of the children, Jacinta and Francisco, would die young, but Lucia would go on to become a Carmelite nun. She died in 2005. All three prayed fervently and made many sacrifices for the conversion of sinners, inspired largely by the vision of Hell that they had been shown. The vision of Hell so affected

Jacinta that years after the vision Mary showed her, she "often sat thoughtfully on the ground or on a rock, and exclaimed: 'Oh, Hell! Hell! How sorry I am for the souls who go to Hell! And the people down there, burning alive, like wood in a fire!'"

Details of what Mary said to the seers have come out slowly, in the form of various letters, interviews, and memoirs. In Sister Lucia's last public interview on 26 December 1957, she told Father Augustin Fuentes:

*"Father, the most Holy Virgin is very sad because no one has paid any attention to Her Message, neither the good nor the bad. The good continue on their way, but without giving any importance to Her Message. The bad, not seeing the punishment of God actually falling upon them, continue their life of sin without even caring about the Message. But believe me, Father, God will chastise the world and this will be in a terrible manner. The punishment from Heaven is imminent.... Russia will be the instrument of chastisement chosen by Heaven to punish the whole world if we do not beforehand obtain the conversion of that poor nation.... my cousins Francisco and Jacinta sacrificed themselves because in all the apparitions of the Most Holy Virgin, they always saw Her very sad. She never smiled at us. This sadness, this anguish which we noted in Her, penetrated our souls. This sadness is caused by the offenses against God and the punishments which menace sinners."* [150]

In November 1917, Freemasons openly barraged the Catholic Church with a number of protests in Rome. They "littered Rome with posters showing the Archangel Michael defeated on the ground trampled beneath a triumphant Lucifer. In their protests against the Catholic Church, the freemasons also displayed the black flag of the heretic Giordano Bruno." [151] Not all was lost, however. On 13 May 1931, in Portugal, a national consecration was made by all the bishops to the Immaculate Heart of Mary. By the time World War II broke out, the country had reversed its course and had swung back to Catholicism, experiencing a rise in not just the laity but also in vocations.

Miraculously, they were spared the ravages of World War II. As of 2011 census data, Portugal is 81% Catholic.

God the Father loves all of mankind. He wants us all in Heaven with Him. He loves us so much that He sent us His only Son to die in redemption for our sins and created for us a heavenly Mother to guide us home, just like any mother would. The Blessed Virgin Mary, the Queen Mother, the spouse of the Holy Spirit, loves every one of us as any mother would. She is sad in part because so many of us are lost to Hell because of sin. But she is also sad because her Son endured the ravages of the cross to redeem those sins, and so many people hurt Him needlessly by continuing to sin. She came to warn us. She came to help us find salvation.

But instead of taking the narrow path to salvation, we got on the highway to Hell.

# XI. A Superhighway for Sin

"The gate is wide and the road broad that leads to destruction, and those who enter through it are many."

AT THE time of the Miracle of the Sun on 13 October 1917, Russia was still ruled by the czar, and the Bolshevik Revolution that saw Lenin and the Communists take power wouldn't happen for twelve more days. When it came, the revolution brought a sweeping change to Russia, but the people hated Communism and Lenin. They still loved Mother Russia and the Orthodox Christian faith.[152] Lenin and the other Communists thought that their revolution would inspire the workers all over the world to rise up and join them, and Communist parties were established in countries around the world. However, they struggled to maintain power in Russia, and a worldwide uprising of the working class simply never happened.

On 17 October 1921, Lenin recognized in a report that the problem he was having getting Communism established in his "worker's paradise" wasn't a military problem but a cultural one. "It is possible to obtain victory in war in a few months," he wrote. "But it is impossible to achieve a cultural victory in such a short time. By its very nature it requires a longer period; and we must adapt ourselves to this longer period, plan our work accordingly, and display the maximum of perseverance, persistence and method."[153] To fix these cultural "problems" of the peasant farmers of Russia, the Communists established Political Education Departments. The determination of the Communists to complete their revolution inside of Russia between 1917 and 1921 resulted in the killing, imprisoning, or starving to death of millions of people, Christian and non-Christian alike.[154]

In 1922, an Italian Neo-Marxist by the name of Antonio Gramsci traveled to Russia as a representative of the new Italian Communist Party. Where Marx perceived that the rich used politics and economics to maintain their power, Gramsci contended that the rich maintained their power by controlling the culture, which he called "cultural hegemony." Gramsci argued that to enact true revolutionary change, there needed to be a change in all facets of culture: arts, movies, schools, magazines and newspapers, and most of all, seminaries. If Marxism was truly to take over, especially the West, Christianity had to be destroyed. Gramsci "considered Christianity to be the 'force binding all the classes—peasants and workers and princes, priests and popes and all the rest besides, into a single, homogeneous culture. It was specifically Christian culture, in which individual men and women understood that the most important things about human life transcend the material conditions in which they lived out their mortal lives.'"[155]

Father James Thornton writes:

*"The civilized world, Gramsci deduced, had been thoroughly saturated with Christianity for 2,000 years and Christianity remains the dominant philosophical and moral system in Europe and North America. Practically speaking, civilization and Christianity were inextricably bound together. Christianity had become so thoroughly integrated into the daily lives of nearly everyone, including non-Christians living in Christian lands, it was so pervasive, that it formed an almost impenetrable barrier to the new, revolutionary civilization Marxists wish to create. Attempting to batter down that barrier proved unproductive, since it only generated powerful counter-revolutionary forces, consolidating them and making them potentially deadly. Therefore, in place of the frontal attack, how much more advantageous and less hazardous it would be to attack the enemy's society subtly, with the aim of transforming the society's collective mind gradually, over a period of a few generations, from its former Christian worldview into one more harmonious to Marxism."[156]*

## MARCHING THROUGH THE INSTITUTIONS

Gramsci's ideas were influential to another group of Neo-Marxists who founded the Institute for Social Research at Goethe University in Frankfurt, Germany, in 1923. This became known as "the Frankfurt School." The Frankfurt School flourished in post-World War I Germany, but when Adolf Hitler became chancellor in 1933, the key members of the Frankfurt School—who were mostly Jewish—realized the threat Hitler posed and relocated. They packed their bags and moved to the United States with the help of the Fabian Society, the Fabian Society-born London School of Economics, and Fabian Socialists at Columbia, Princeton, and other universities in the United States.[157] The Frankfurt School saw the problems Lenin was having in Russia and realized he and Gramsci had identified the two types of revolution: political, and cultural. Where political revolution was about taking control of the government and the economy, cultural revolution was about winning the hearts and minds of large swaths of society by means of altering how the masses perceived change. By separating the cultural from the economic and political, it would be possible to make cultural Marxists out of people who rejected Marxism on political grounds. The Frankfurt School, then, focused their efforts on cultural revolution through changes in media, education, popular culture, sex, and most importantly, the traditional family. Members of the Frankfurt School "preached that 'Even a partial breakdown of parental authority in the family might tend to increase the readiness of a coming generation to accept social change.'"[158]

When Our Lady of Fatima forewarned that Russia would spread her errors around the world, we had no way of knowing what form they would take. And we certainly had no idea that the epicenter of transmission of the errors would move from Communist Russia, to Germany, to the United States; from Marx and Engels, to Lenin, to Frankfurt, to New York City. When the Frankfurt School reached the rich soil of the land of the free in the 1930's, Satan's ivy of misperception *really* began to grow. Timothy Matthews, writing about the Frankfurt School for *Catholic Insight* in March of 2009, stated that the task of the Frankfurt School was to as swiftly as possible "undermine the Judaeo-Christian legacy. To do this they called for the most negative destructive criticism possible of every sphere of life which would be designed to de-stabilize society and bring down what they saw as the 'oppressive' order."[159]

The Frankfurt School's notable members—Herbert Marcuse, Theodor Adorno, Max Horkheimer, Wilhelm Reich, Leo Lowenthal, Walter Benjamin, Erich Fromm, Ludwig Wittgenstein, Jurgen Habermas, Abraham Maslow, Carl Rogers, Lord Bertrand Russel, Dr. Timothy Leary, and Noam Chomsky, to name a few—regularly published books, papers, and articles, lectured and charted the course for the future of academics at numerous colleges in the United States. Far from having a centralized organizational structure, the Frankfurt School was more of a loose knit collection of free thinkers who at times disagreed about the means but had a very common end. By blending the goals of Marx with the sexual psychology of Freud, the School's "Critical Theory" was a euphemism for what they were really out to achieve: a Cultural Marxist revolution.

Herbert Marcuse summed up their thinking quite succinctly: "The traditional idea of revolution and the traditional strategy of revolution have ended. These ideas are old-fashioned … what we must undertake is a type of diffuse and dispersed disintegration of the system."[160] So, with their eyes focused on the long goal of cultural revolution, the Frankfurt School set about enacting pervasive cultural changes in five key areas.

1.   Education

In education, adherents to the Frankfurt School taught people to perceive that the influence of parents and the home are obstructive to true learning. Lord Bertrand Russell advocated for the same thing the Freemasons did: to capture the youth, saying that "not much can be done unless indoctrination begins before the age of ten."[161] Building on the philosophers who came before him, Russell said that "education should aim at destroying free will, so that, after pupils have left school, they shall be incapable, throughout the rest of their lives, of thinking or acting otherwise than as their schoolmasters would have wished."[162] The ideas of "political correctness" and "tolerance" all sprung from the Frankfurt School. It should also be noted that the "psychotherapeutic classroom," "outcome based education," "sensitivity training," and "encounter groups" are also results of the Frankfurt School.

2.  Entertainment

Russell, again, summed up the thinking of the Frankfurt School when it came to the power that entertainment in general, and movies in particular, have over altering the perceptions of wide swaths of the population:

*"The great majority of young people in almost all civilized countries derive their ideas of love, of honour [sic], of the way to make money, and of the importance of good clothes, from the evenings spent in seeing what Hollywood thinks good for them. I doubt whether all the schools and churches combined have as much influence as the cinema upon the opinions of the young in regard to such intimate matters as love and marriage and money-making. The producers of Hollywood are the high-priests of a new religion."[163]*

Theodor Adorno wrote in his essay "On the Social Situation of Music" that music can serve as a "call for change through the coded language of suffering." The "social cement" of society, as he called it, could be leveraged to effect sweeping cultural change. Members of the Frankfurt School influenced the development of not just movies and popular music, but also art, advertising, and the portrayal of news.

3.  Drugs

Many in the Frankfurt School believed that the use of hallucinogenic drugs was a necessary component to achieving their plans. Aldous Huxley, famed author of *A Brave New World*, "proceeded to initiate a network of drug researchers and aficionados that included Timothy Leary, Ken Kesey, and Jerry Garcia."[164] Huxley believed that the biggest impediment to mass adoption of what he called "brain drugs" was the Bible. Timothy Leary explained, "We had run up against the Judeo-Christian commitment to one God, one religion, one reality, that has cursed Europe for centuries and America since our founding days. Drugs that open the mind to multiple realities inevitably lead to a polytheistic view of the universe. We sensed that the time for a new humanist religion based on intelligence, good-natured pluralism and scientific paganism had arrived."[165] In his 1968 book *The Politics of Ecstasy,* Leary said "If you are serious about your religion, if you really wish to commit yourself to the spiritual quest, you must learn how to use psychochemicals. Drugs are the religion of the twenty-first century."

4. Sex

It seems all members of the Frankfurt School were adamant that there simply had to be a revolution in how society perceived sex and issues surrounding it, namely birth control, abortion, illegitimate children, and population control. They envisioned a society where the greatest satisfactions in life are all sexual. Wilhelm Reich, according to *Marxists.org,* "developed his own doctrine of sexual liberalism as an antidote to political conformism,"[166] and he "praised the undermining of patriarchal authority."[167] It was Reich who coined the term "sexual revolution" in a book he authored in 1936 by the same name. In it, he criticized the suppression of sexuality in children, the repression of sexual freedom in adolescents, the stigma of abnormal sexual desires such as homosexuality, the illegality of abortion, monogamous marriage, marriage as an institution, and the difficulty of divorce. His views were supported by fellow Frankfurt School member Bertrand Russell, who complained that the "fear doctrine" of Christianity repressed the natural drive to satisfy sexual appetites. Another member, Herbert Marcuse, wrote *Eros and Civilization* in 1955, which appealed to college students in the "free love" period of the 1960s, closing its preface of the 1966 edition with its message that "the fight for life, the fight for Eros, is the *political* fight."[168] (Emphasis in original.)

5. The Family

The Frankfurt School members universally felt the traditional family—made of a monogamous husband and wife—was an outdated impediment to the progress of society. They argued that the traditional Christian hierarchy, with the man as head of the family, served only to create neuroses in their children by repressing their natural urges. The family represented an obstacle to society's adoption of a more "enlightened" way of thinking, a way that prioritized basic human desires over obstacles such as the "myth" of religion and the "forced morality" that came with it. They saw marriage as a prison, where those inside were trapped and repressed, serving only as a "factory for authoritarian ideologies" for future generations. In his book *The Sexual Revolution,* Wilhelm Reich said, "As miserable and hopeless, painful and intolerable as the marital situation and family constellation may be, the members of the family must defend it, in the family and outside. The social necessity of doing so makes it necessary to hush up the actual misery and to idealize family and marriage..."[169] "...we do not consider the family the cornerstone and basis of society, but the product of its economic structure."[170] Reich stressed that society would fail to accept a collectivist—that is to say, Communist—way of life "unless the children enter collective education before they are in a position to form these destructive attachments to the parents, that is, before the fourth year of life."[171]

## THE ERRORS OF RUSSIA

Our Lady of Fatima told the three shepherd children that Russia would spread her errors around the world. Using a wide-angle lens, we can see that all the efforts of Satan over the years from 1884 to today are embodied in the Errors of Russia, and they all contribute to the same ultimate goal: *The complete destruction of the traditional family.*

How would this look? Far from being a myth or a far-off idea of a handful of intellectuals, it was actually tried on a wide scale. In Russia. In July of 1926, *The Atlantic* published an article, "The Russian Effort to Abolish Marriage" that gave us a detailed look:

*"When the Bolsheviki came into power in 1917 they regarded the family, like every other 'bourgeois' institution, with fierce hatred, and set out with a will to destroy it. 'To clear the family out of the accumulated dust of the ages we had to give it a good shakeup, and we did,' declared Madame Smidovich, a leading Communist and active participant in the recent discussion. So one of the first decrees of the Soviet Government abolished the term 'illegitimate children.' This was done simply by equalizing the legal status of all children, whether born in wedlock or out of it, and now the Soviet Government boasts that Russia is the only country where there are no illegitimate children.... At the same time a law was passed which made divorce a matter of a few minutes, to be obtained at the request of either partner in a marriage. Chaos was the result. Men took to changing wives with the same zest which they displayed in the consumption of the recently restored forty-percent vodka.... Peasants with a respectable married life of forty years and more behind them suddenly decided to leave their wives and remarry. Peasant boys looked upon marriage as an exciting game and changed wives with the change of seasons. It was not an unusual occurrence for a boy of twenty to have had three or four wives, or for a girl of the same age to have had three or four abortions.... Krilenko, the Soviet public prosecutor, who had a very large share in the framing of the bill and is one of its most passionate advocates, argued that there is neither necessity, importance, nor even utility in the registration of a marriage. 'Why*

*should the State know who marries whom?' he exclaimed. 'Of course, if living together and not registration is taken as the test of a married state, polygamy and polyandry may exist; but the State can't put up any barriers against this. Free love is the ultimate aim of a socialist State; in that State marriage will be free from any kind of obligation, including economic, and will turn into an absolutely free union of two beings.'"* [172]

The goals of the Frankfurt School are the same goals that Friedrich Engels outlined in 1884. They have the same attitude toward marriage as was held by Vladimir Lenin. They advocate the same tactics used by the Freemasons and the Fabian Socialists. What the Frankfurt School was doing wasn't new. It wasn't blazing a new trail. No, it was simply making the road wider. It was making it even easier to fall away to vice. It was making it more socially acceptable to walk away from the Domestic Church. The ivy of misperception had succeeded in doing its job.

Traditional families teach traditional values such as religion to their children. Traditional families embody the sacrifice of spouses for each other, and of parents for their children. They model virtue, avoid vice, love God, adore Jesus Christ, and desire an eternity in Heaven. They obey the word of God, and follow the teachings of Jesus Christ and His apostles. Their eyes are fixed on the goal of eternal life, not the life of this earth. In short, traditional families—the Domestic Church—are the embodiment of everything Satan wants to destroy. The Errors of Russia are Satan's means to that evil end. And there can be no doubt that he's been waging a successful campaign to destroy the Domestic Church.

# XII. Trainwreck of Emotions

"And if a house is divided against itself,
that house will not be able to stand."

Mark 3:25

# XII. Trainwreck of Emotions

SATAN works by creating doubt about truth, creating fear about everything good, and distorting everything beautiful with lies. He causes us to question how we perceive God, sin, and the intentions of other people. These are the roots of his ivy of misperception, his false vine, his lies. He has been using these means to slowly attack one Domestic Church after another, with the end goal of destroying Christ's Church. Today, Satan is reaping the rewards of centuries of labor. Before, we could rely on our faith and the strength of the Domestic Church to prevent our emotions from overwhelming us. However, since Satan planted the ivy of misperception around the Domestic Church eight hundred years ago, the damage has made us vulnerable to attacks using our emotions against us. The only thing Satan has access to is imagination and emotions, and because of the damage of the ivy of misperception, Satan is now able to easily manipulate the **Four Emotions of Division:** Fear, Hate, Confusion, and Apathy. These Four Emotions of Division work to divide the Domestic Church against itself, and widen the divide between people and God.

## FEAR

Fear is one of the most primal emotions, experienced even by animals. Fear has the ability to override all manner of logic and reason, and in a hyper-excited state can override even the most basic drivers of behavior, such as hunger or thirst. Satan subtly and skillfully manipulates our perceptions to stir up the emotion of fear. Fear can make us do something he wants, or prevent us from doing something he doesn't. When Satan wants to leverage fear, his attacks on our perceptions typically focus on fears associated with earthly forms of success, material goods, and earthly pleasures: our career, possessions, and activities.

As children, we are taught to fear rather than trust. For example, even though the occurrences of kidnapping and crimes against children are on the decline, we are taught to be afraid of adults who are not family.

Before we enter our teens, we are instilled with the fear that if we don't go to college that we'll have a miserable life. What's more, we're told it had better be the *right* college and *right* degree, regardless of how much it costs and how much of a burden that college debt will create down the line. Teens are also encouraged to fear that their parents are holding them back due to their "backward, unenlightened" thinking. There's also the fear of not having a good enough job, and once we have that job, there's the fear that we're not going to do anything important and all the effort and money and sacrifice of college and late nights at the office will be for nothing.

While all this is going on, we're urged—by every form of media—to find our soulmate. "Don't settle," we're told. "Don't compromise. Enjoy your season of singleness. Find meaning in your wait to find The One. Better to wait than settle down too soon." As the average age of marriage has increased over 30% since 1955, we get more entrenched in the careers that now define us. We put off marriage out of a fear that The One, our "bigger, better deal" will come along *after* we're married to someone who is less perfect than The One. Most people also have friends or relatives who had a bad marriage and got divorced (or are products of broken homes themselves) which leads to fear of divorce before even getting married. Of course, at some point the fear of *not* being married causes most people to just pick the best option that's available and get married before it's too late to have kids.

Once we're finally married, there's a new set of fears that hit us. By now, deeply established in our careers, we have the fear of getting the right house in the right neighborhood with the right schools for the kids we don't have yet. And the kids! Of course, there are fears about having kids. When is the right time to have them? How will we pay for them? How will having kids impact the lifestyle and careers we've spent most of our young lives creating? Once we overcome the fear of having children and finally get pregnant, even more fears are heaped on us, like the fear that if we don't eat the right things or play the right music for our unborn baby he will somehow be disadvantaged. So our baby is born and we are handed a whole host of new fears: lead paint, poisonous cleaners, BPA plastics, gluten, GMO and non-organic foods, pesticides, herbicides.... The natural desire to be protective of our precious children is turned into fear of everything around us.

We're also driven by the fear of what other people think of us, our lives, and our children, so we do our best to maintain an online social media persona of a perfect life, with perfect pictures and stories of our exciting activities and achievements. Social media drives the fear that we will be harshly judged by *everyone* if we don't live up to some impossible yet invisible standard. So, since our kids are a reflection of ourselves, we simply cannot allow them to be perceived by our social media circle to be unsuccessful in life. Therefore we make sure we get our kids into every extracurricular activity as soon as it's available, in some cases as young as two years old. Every one of these activities has a variety of camps available over the summers: music camps, robotics camps, sports camps, science camps, art camps, and many others. We are petrified by the fear that if our children aren't attending all of the same camps as their peers and performing at a high level from the time they can crawl, they'll fall behind their classmates, never get into a good school, never have a good career, and never be successful.

We also fear looking old, feeling old, and being perceived as old. We fear retirement and not having enough money. And most of all, we're afraid of dying, so we as a society spend an estimated $1.2 *trillion* dollars globally every year in the supplement, pharmaceutical, and fitness industries combined.

Of course, we pass all these fears onto our own kids, just as they were passed along to us.

## HATE

Though fear might be more powerful, hate is a more evil and more Satanic emotion. We know that Satan hates God's perfections, holiness, and justice. He hates marriage and he hates children because he hates all of mankind. Wherever there is hate, there is Satan. And he wants us to hate too. So he twists our perceptions of other people, their lives, and their motives to grow our hatred toward each other and ourselves.

As a society, we have come to hate people who aren't like us, because Satan has been successful at dividing us into little groups of people who hate each other. As a result, we hate other people because of the color of their skin. We hate other people because of what nation they come from, what language they speak, or the regional traditions they practice. We hate other people for how their bodies look, or because of things their ancestors did or did not do. We hate other people because of their social status, their income level, or their profession. We hate people who are more successful than us and scorn those who are less successful. We hate other people because of their parents, their family, or their gender. Some even hate people who have disabilities or who are elderly because all they see are non-contributing drains on the resources of society. We, as a society, have come to hate other people because of *how God made them and how God blesses them,* which is not anything that is controlled by people as individuals but by our Creator. But even all that hate isn't enough for Satan.

Satan even causes us to hate ourselves. Because of Satan, we are told we should hate the color of our own skin, and how our bodies look at every age. We are told we should hate where we come from, and who our ancestors were. We are told we should hate our own gender, that we should hate our own sexuality, and that we should hate ourselves for what we can't do as well as other people. We are told that we should hate our failures and our inability to live up to earthly ideals that are nothing but lies, to begin with. We are told that we should hate where we are in our state in life, no matter where that is. We should even hate the very thoughts we have about what is right and what is wrong, because it's our own thoughts that cause everyone else to hate us. In short, we are told that we should hate the way God made us and hate the Creator for making us who we are. For some people, this hatred of self leads to the tragedy of suicide.

## CONFUSION

With all the fear and hate, the end result is the creation within us of another emotion: confusion. As our perceptions of what is good, true, and beautiful are manipulated, we find ourselves confused between conflicting emotions and wavering perceptions of what is truth. We are conditioned to fear marriage yet hate ourselves for being single and hate those who are happily married. (Or at least *seem* to be happily married, according to their social media posts.) We are conditioned to fear the responsibilities that come with the job of being a parent, yet when we take our kids to daycare we hate that we don't spend more time with them. We fear the loss of income that would come with dropping to a one-income family and hate that it feels like we have no other option than to be a two-income family. We fear that we're doing it all wrong and hate that it seems like everyone else is doing the same things and seems to be doing it all right.

On top of all this, the state of marriage as an institution seems to change daily. There's constant arguing over whether it's strictly a religious matter, strictly a civil matter, or some combination of both. There are those who fight to maintain the definition of marriage, and those who fight to change that definition. Among those who are fighting to change the definition, there's little agreement about what the "new definition of marriage" should be. Protestant denominations have further split and splintered over this issue. For Satan, the confusion over the definition of marriage isn't enough. Today, men and women are both confused about their roles in marriage and what the "proper" expressions of masculinity and femininity are, because there are so many conflicting messages all designed to affect our perceptions of truth and leave us bewildered.

And it doesn't end there: children are growing up more confused than ever. Even if they are raised in a traditional family, they are bombarded with confusing and conflicting messages about what marriage is, who can get married, and what makes up a family. Children are also being told that they can choose to be whatever gender they want to be, with some children being raised in "gender neutral households" by parents who say they don't want to force gender identity or sexual orientation stereotypes on their children. In schools, in the media, and online, they are also encouraged to distrust and challenge their parents, who try to teach them right from wrong on these and other issues of faith and morals. By the time they are in their early twenties, most children are like ships with no sail and no rudder, trying to navigate in the world without a solid foundation in faith and lacking trust and respect for their parents.

## APATHY

The constant barrage of fear, hate, and resulting confusion drives a lot of people to simply "check out." Many people reach a point at which they're tired of fighting against the fear, exhausted from fighting the hate, and weary of being confused. It's far easier to just stop caring than to keep struggling, especially when they feel like their entire day is spent fighting. They feel like this because their entire day is spent fighting the attacks of Satan, and this is by his design. And, also by Satan's design, they find their escape in any number of vices that are readily available. Of course, Satan has distorted the perception of what is and isn't a sin, so most of these vices aren't even viewed as wrong by most people. In many cases, these vices trigger a chemical in the brain called dopamine, which has been linked to almost every kind of addictive behavior. Timothy Leary's advice from the 1960's to "turn on, tune in, drop out" has never been easier, or more addictive.

Can there be any doubt that we have become increasingly an apathetic society? Millions of people worldwide spend countless hours playing video games that desensitize them to violence, morals, and consequences. When the games aren't distracting us, we switch to endless hours of social media. Our TV-watching habits are so consuming that we have coined terms like "binge watching" and "Netflix and chill" to describe them. The constant barrage of fear, hate, and confusion has led to millions of people having anxiety disorders, panic attacks, and ADHD. To treat these problems, we are prescribed a wide array of medications that turn us into people who are numb to the world and the people around us. If we skip the doctor and choose to self-medicate to escape, we can start with legalized marijuana. Of course, if that doesn't get the job done it's not difficult to switch to something a little more powerful, like opioids, heroin, crack, crystal meth, or prescription medications obtained illegally, all of which are easily accessible. Or maybe we decide to head off to another increasingly common wonderland of escape: a casino. With every wager to escape the fear, hate, and confusion in our lives, Satan buys us another round of drinks on the house and doubles down on his success in destroying us. And of course, if your spouse is getting you down, there's always the escape of app-enabled adultery or a never-ending stream of pornography on the smartphone in your pocket.

When husbands become apathetic, they abandon their God-given role as leaders of their families. When wives become apathetic, they abandon their role as the heart of the family. Regardless of which one abandons his role first, the other is left to struggle on his own until he too becomes apathetic. As a result, the children are left with no leadership and no heart, adrift to emotionally and spiritually raise themselves. For Satan, they have become easy prey.

### ASSESSING THE DAMAGE

The only fear we should have is the fear of losing eternal life. We should only hate the one who tempts us and the sins we commit when we fail to resist those temptations. We should never be confused about what is true, good, or beautiful. Yet here we are, fearing what is temporary, hating the work of the Creator, and so apathetic we no longer recognize anything beautiful. We have completely inverted God's created order so that our emotions and the failed perceptions that generate them rule over right reason.

It is natural to think that it's not *that* bad. We never like to hear the really bad news, the news that there's a monster in the room with us. We prefer to put our fingers in our ears and close our eyes, repeating the comforting lie "there are no such things as monsters" over and over again until the truth sounds impossible.

Until you open your eyes and realize the ugly monster of reality is still standing there. *And you force yourself to look.*

# XIII. Rubble

"They exchanged the truth of God for a lie
and revered and worshiped the creature
rather than the creator, who is blessed forever."

Romans 1:25

# XIII. Rubble

O N 2 FEBRUARY 1995, in the Italian city of Civitavecchia, five-year-old Jessica Gregori witnessed tears of blood streaming from the eyes of the statue of the Blessed Mother her family had placed in their garden grotto just the year before. Her father and other witnesses saw the blood tears that day and on 12 more occasions in the days after the initial event. Their bishop remained skeptical. On the 15th of March, the bishop's sister asked him to join her in prayer at this statue, and he agreed. While praying the Salve Regina, when they reached the words "Turn then, most gracious Advocate, thine eyes of mercy toward us," the statue began to weep blood for the fourteenth time. The bishop had the statue taken to Rome for investigation. The tears were found to be of a male in his mid-thirties, and multiple scans showed that there were no hidden tubes or apparatuses that would cause the tears. While the Vatican retained possession of the original statue, Pope John Paul II sent a cardinal on 10 April 1995, to present a replacement statue to the family as a gift. The replacement was carved by the original artist and was otherwise identical to the original. The replacement soon began to emit a fragrant scent on liturgical feast days, and on several occasions— including 2 April 2005, the day Pope John Paul II died—it wept human tears. But this was not all.

Beginning on 2 July 1995, and continuing for almost a year, the Gregori family began to experience apparitions of the Blessed Mother, who presented herself as "Queen of the Church and Queen of the family." The bishop was again skeptical of the family's claims, and so he asked young Jessica Gregori the next time she saw an apparition to ask the Blessed Virgin to provide her a fact about himself that only he knew. Jessica returned with not one, but several facts about the bishop. The bishop's skepticism vanished.

During the apparitions, the Blessed Mother gave many messages to the family. Fabio Gregori, patriarch of the family, said, "there will be the great combat to destroy the Christian family, the great family of

God, the Church, and diminishing his full Word and the Eucharist with apostolic communion."[173] The Blessed Mother also told them, "My children, the darkness of Satan is now obscuring the whole world and it is also obscuring the Church of God. Prepare to live what I had revealed to my little daughters of Fatima."[174] Then on 27 August 1995, Jessica was given the Third Secret of Fatima by the Blessed Mother. The next year while on a pilgrimage to Fatima, Jessica was able to visit Sister Lucia, (which was highly unusual given the fact that Sister Lucia lived in a cloistered convent and had almost no contact with the outside world,) and the two discussed the Third Secret in private. Then on 16 July 1996, the Blessed Mother told the Gregori family that "Satan wants to destroy the family." The messages regarding Our Lady's repeated warnings about Satan's attack on the family didn't stop there.

## THE FINAL BATTLE

In 2008, Cardinal Caffarra was interviewed after celebrating Mass. During the interview, he explained that Pope John Paul II had instructed him to form the Pontifical Institute for Studies on Marriage and Family. At the beginning of this endeavor, he wrote a letter to Sister Lucia, one of the three children of Fatima, through her bishop, since according to the rules of her order, she could not be contacted directly. He asked in the letter for her prayers and did not expect a response. He was surprised when he received a long letter of reply from Sister Lucia:

*"'In that letter we find written: "The final battle between the Lord and the kingdom of Satan will be about Marriage and the Family." Don't be afraid, she added, because whoever works for the sanctity of Marriage and the Family will always be fought against and opposed in every way, because this is the decisive issue. Then she concluded: "nevertheless, Our Lady has already crushed his head".' Cardinal Caffarra added that 'speaking again with John Paul II, you could feel that the family was the core, since it has to do with the supporting pillar of creation, the truth of the relationship between man and woman,*

*between the generations. If the foundational pillar is damaged, the entire building collapses and we're seeing this now, because we are right at this point and we know it.'"* [175]

What is left of our society? What is left of the Domestic Church? What is left of the walls? Who is left inside? How much damage has the ivy of misperception done?

**PROPHESIES OF OUR LADY OF GOOD SUCCESS**
"Often, during this epoch the enemies of Jesus Christ, instigated by the Devil, will steal consecrated Hosts from the churches so that they might profane the Eucharistic Species."

> On 7 May 2019, a user of online retailer Etsy posted for sale, "Real Catholic Hosts, consecrated by a priest!!! 9 pieces***!!! Made in Germany! Black Mass Magic Satanism". In the description, the seller described their use as "to abuse for classic black fairs or black magic purposes." When contacted anonymously by a journalist who inquired as to their authenticity, the seller replied, "Maybe you don't know, but to celebrate an authentic black mass, you have to be an ordained Catholic priest.... There are a handful of priests in Germany who work in the satanic underground." [176] In the overnight hours of June 16-17th at St. Elizabeth of the Hill Country Catholic Church in Boone, North Carolina, thieves broke in and stole the tabernacle with the Blessed Sacrament inside. Parish cantor Matthew Mellon told a reporter, "I dare speculate that the thief had demonic intentions because many lighter valuable items were passed over, including a jeweled monstrance, in the sanctuary." [177]

"As for the Sacrament of Matrimony, which symbolizes the union of Christ with His Church, it will be attacked and profaned in the fullest sense of the word."

> In a video interview in 2013, Dutch homosexual activist Boris Dittrich said that now that the redefinition of marriage has

succeeded in convincing people to accept homosexual "marriages" as equal to traditional marriages, the acceptance of group marriages made up of three or more people is the next logical step. [178] Seven years later, on 25 June 2020, the Massachusetts town of Somerville became the first in the nation to make polyamorous relationships legally recognized by unanimous city council vote. [179]

## "Innocence will almost no longer be found in children, nor modesty in women"

During the state-mandated stay-at-home and quarantine orders caused by the coronavirus in 2020, Teen Vogue also gave tips and tricks to its readers on the practice of "sexting" or sending nude or semi-nude photographs via text. It told its readers that "Sexting should make you feel good," and "Like anything worth doing, sexting takes practice." [180] On 25 March 2019, *The Observer*—a student newspaper for Notre Dame, Saint Mary's, and Holy Cross colleges—published a letter to the editor penned by Maryann White. In it, she criticized the wearing of yoga pants or leggings outside the gym in general and to Mass in particular. "I was at Mass at the Basilica with my family. In front of us was a group of young women, all wearing very snug-fitting leggings and all wearing short-waisted tops (so that the lower body was uncovered except for the leggings). Some of them truly looked as though the leggings had been painted on them." [181] The letter sparked outrage: on campus, over 1,400 female students—almost 25% of the 5,794 female students in that school year [182]—responded by pledging to participate in "The Leggings Protest" and wore leggings everywhere for over two days. [183] Student replies to *The Observer*, social media, and news outlets around the country joined the chorus of those criticizing the mother's letter.

## FREEMASONS

"Let us, then, not make martyrs, but let us popularize vice among the multitudes. Let us cause them to draw it in by their five senses; to drink it in; to be saturated with it."

In the early 1990s only six states offered commercial casinos. That figure tripled by 2013, with a total of 30 states offering some form of legalized gambling.[184] Since 2012, ten states have legalized recreational marijuana, with proposed legislation making its way through several other states.[185] In 2019, lawmakers in several states introduced legislation to decriminalize prostitution.[186] The world's largest free porn site boasted that it received over 33,500,000,000 site visits during 2018 alone, transferring 4,403,000,000,000 megabytes of data.[187] That's 92 million *daily* average visits, using more bandwidth per day than the entire internet consumed in the entire year of 2002.

"Our final end is that of Voltaire and of the French Revolution, the destruction forever of Catholicism and even of the Christian idea which, if left standing on the ruins of Rome, would be the resuscitation of Christianity later on."

At the July 1992 celebration of the reunification of Mexican Freemasonry in Mexico City, Grand Master Francisco Valle Guzman condemned the Catholic Church as "the most powerful and ruthless enemy of science, progress, civilization, fraternity, and love. Any reconciliation between us is impossible."[188] According to Gallup data, in 1955, 73% of American Catholics aged 21-29 attended Mass at least weekly. Just prior to the coronavirus pandemic, that figure was down to 25%.[189] Even among older Americans, Mass attendance is on the decline, with the 60 and older demographic of weekly Mass goers dropping below 50%. According to the Gallup report, "For the first time, a majority of Catholics in no generational group attend weekly."[190] The decline is not unique to the Catholic Church: according to a 2019 article in *The Daily Mail*, Protestant Christian denominations have seen a 62.5% decline since 1982, while those who claim no religious affiliation at all has risen a staggering 266% between 1988 and 2018.[191]

"[The Freemasons] will conquer the Catholic Church not by argumentation, but rather with moral corruption."—St. Maximilian Kolbe on the Freemasonic objective

"A Barna Research Group survey found that a majority of teenagers believe that 'not recycling' ranks as worse on the immorality scale than viewing porn."[192] "Studies now prove that pornography and other sexualized media have the capacity to alter drastically the user's brain chemistry and functionality, sometimes leading to addiction. Even if a person does not become addicted, they are impacted by the mental, emotional, and spiritual effects of viewing pornography. These effects can lead to marital strain or divorce for married adults, relationship and intimacy problems and, for children, a permanently warped view of women and sexual intimacy."[193] Dr. Victor B. Cline, clinical psychologist at the University of Utah with a private practice specializing in family and marital counseling observed, "Pornography which was originally perceived as shocking, taboo-breaking, illegal, repulsive, or immoral, though still sexually arousing, in time came to be seen as acceptable and commonplace.... There is an increasing sense that 'everybody does it' and this gave them permission to also do it, even though the activity was possibly illegal and contrary to their previous moral beliefs and personal standards."[194] Sociologist Samuel L. Perry did a study on the effects of pornography on conservative Protestants. He found that "[a]fter looking at pornography for a long enough time, they started to back away from their faith a little bit. They were less likely to pray, less likely to attend church, less likely to feel like God is playing an important part in their lives."[195] In a 2020 op-ed for political and culture news website *The Daily Beast,* former Disney *Boy Meets World* star Maitland Ward commented on her departure from mainstream media for the world of adult films: "It's time for porn to be mainstream and mainstream to accept porn."[196]

"It is to the youth we must go. It is that which we must seduce."

One study shows that among college-age males, 49% were first introduced to pornography before the age of 13, and 93% had seen internet pornography during adolescence; 64% of people age 13-24 actively seek out pornography at least once a week.[197] "Many children stumble upon explicit material while doing otherwise innocent internet searches, doing homework, or simply by opening email. According to statistics compiled by GuardChild, 70% of children ages 7 to 18 years old have inadvertently been exposed to online pornography. Some ... report first encountering pornography at the age of 5 or 6."[198] Dr. Jill Manning, author of *What's the Big Deal About Pornography? A Guide for the Internet Generation,* says "I believe pornography is the most successfully marketed insult and attack on our divine nature as human beings that has ever existed. There's never been anything so calculated and widespread and so effective at reaching so many people at such a young age."[199] And if, thanks to our hyper-sexualized culture, a teenage girl becomes pregnant and wants an abortion, magazines targeted to teens such as *Teen Vogue* tell young girls not only how to obtain an abortion without their parents' knowledge, but says that the anti-abortion views of some parents are "abstract," that "having access to abortion should be your right," and that "everybody loves someone who's had an abortion."[200]

## Socialists

"If you can't justify your existence ... then, clearly, we cannot use the organizations of our society for the purpose of keeping you alive, because your life does not benefit us and it can't be of very much use to yourself."—George Bernard Shaw

In George Bernard Shaw's home country of England, the National Healthcare System (NHS) routinely uses a panel of bureaucrats to approve or deny medications and treatment to patients. One example of the effect of this system comes from research conducted in 2010 that showed as many as 20,000 cancer patients had their lives cut short by drug rationing.[201] According to *The Daily Mail*, the NHS intentionally kills 130,000 patients every year by placing them on an "assisted death pathway" in an effort to cut costs and free up hospital beds.[202] But it's not just the elderly: it's also sick babies, who are denied food and water until they die.[203] In the United States, the Affordable Care Act— frequently referred to as ObamaCare—initially had language that would have established a 15-member Independent Payment Advisory Board that would have determined which procedures and medications would and would not be covered. The backlash caused this part of the Affordable Care Act to be removed, but that doesn't mean the efforts to establish such "death panels" have stopped. The non-profit Institute for Clinical and Economic Review (ICER) is establishing "value frameworks" that it is promoting to help health insurers lower costs by denying coverage. It has already been partially accepted by the Veteran's Administration, healthcare insurer CVS Caremark, and New York State's Medicaid program, with Medicare Part D (which covers approximately 43 million senior citizens) indicating they might start using the ICER frameworks starting in 2020.[204] And in Canada, their Supreme Court ruled in 2013 that a group of people appointed by the government could choose to end the life of anyone on life support who they arbitrarily decide is "terminal" in an effort to reduce costs to their single-payer healthcare system.[205]

# XIII. Rubble

"A great many people would have to be put out of existence simply because it wastes other people's time to look after them."—George Bernard Shaw

As part of a series of regular questions asked to mothers who are expecting, doctors routinely ask if there are any problems with the pregnancy, would the mother want to keep the baby. Later in the pregnancy, mothers are encouraged to undergo prenatal genetic screening, and depending on the results of the tests, the mothers are encouraged to "discuss options." As a result, an estimated 92% of mothers in the United States who receive a prenatal diagnosis that their unborn child has Down syndrome have an abortion,[206] despite the fact that prenatal tests can be wrong 50% or more of the time.[207] In Iceland, mothers who have abortions after being told the prenatal genetic screening test indicated their unborn child might have Down syndrome is almost 100%.[208] On the other end of the spectrum of life, governments have also intervened to legally permit euthanasia in the famed cases of Terri Schiavo in the United States in 2005 and Alfie Evans in England in 2018. In France in 2019, the fate of 42-year-old Vincent Lambert was determined by the European Court of Human Rights. He was a brain damaged quadriplegic after an accident, but breathed on his own, could swallow (though he was fed through a feeding tube), would respond to his name by turning his head, and follow people around the room with his eyes. Yet after the court's final ruling, his feeding tube was removed and he died nine days later of starvation. Euthanasia is easily procured in Holland and Belgium, and seven states in the United States have so-called "death with dignity" acts passed into law. According to the Washington State Department of Health's "2018 Death with Dignity Act Report," the number of Washington state residents who have procured doctor assisted suicide since the act passed into law in 2009 has risen 424%.[209]

"[W]hen we realize that each feeble-minded person is a potential source of an endless progeny of defect, we prefer the policy of immediate sterilization, of making sure that parenthood is absolutely prohibited to the feeble-minded."—Margaret Sanger

The founder of the American Birth Control League—later renamed Planned Parenthood—was both a socialist and a eugenicist who believed in ridding the human race of what she called "inferiors": people with low IQ, mental illness, African-Americans, Italians, Jews, Irish, Slavs, Hispanics, Asians, Native Americans, and more. In a 1927 opinion, Supreme Court Justice Oliver Wendell Holmes, Jr. legitimized compulsory sterilization. Many states enacted mandatory sterilization programs which operated through the early 1980s, sterilizing as many as 65,000 Americans without their consent, some without their knowledge.[210] Today, the programs for *forced* sterilization have ended, but depending on where you live, you may qualify for *free* sterilization, paid for by the state. For example, the state of Washington started a program in 1997 that provided free vasectomies to low-income residents. As of this writing, residents in Washington State who are on Medicaid qualify for taxpayer-funded sterilization of both men and women,[211] and due to language in the Affordable Care Act (ObamaCare), voluntary sterilization is a covered contraception method nationwide. Because of this, starting 1 August 2012, girls as young as fifteen can be sterilized in the state of Oregon without parental knowledge or consent.[212] If sterilization of "inferiors" isn't possible, encouraging or even forcing them to have abortions has become the next go-to. For example, on 21 June 2019, in England, a court ruled that a Catholic woman with developmental disabilities who was 22 weeks pregnant would be forced to have an abortion for "her best interests," despite the fact that the woman's own mother stated she would raise the baby.[213]

## COMMUNISTS

"After the earthly family is discovered to be the secret of the holy family, the former must then itself be destroyed in theory and in practice"—Karl Marx

On 19 May 2012, author and outspoken LGBT activist Masha Gessen was at the Sydney Writer's Festival on a panel titled, "Why Get Married When You Can be Happy." About six and a half minutes into the discussion, she said, "It's a no-brainer that the institution of marriage should not exist. (Applause) ... Fighting for gay marriage generally involves lying about what we're going to do with marriage when we get there, because we lie that the institution of marriage is not going to change, and that is a lie. The institution of marriage is going to change and it should change, and again I don't think it should exist."[214] Gessen is far from alone in her thinking. Another person leading the charge for change is author and activist Sophie Lewis. In her 2019 book *Full Surrogacy Now: Feminism Against Family*, she envisions a world where women who choose to have babies are employed in the occupational field of "gestational labor," and that it's important to "de-naturalize the mother-child bond." She goes on to challenge "the idea that babies belong to anyone," and criticizes the nuclear family for "training us up to be workers, training us to be inhabitants of a binary-gendered and racially stratified system, training us not to be queer."[215] In a video released by her publisher, she goes on to defend abortion as "a form of killing that we need to be able to defend" as an acceptable form of violence by a "gestator" who wants to go on strike or exit the "gestator workplace."[216] These women are not alone in their sentiments, but are rater just two examples of today's many outspoken Marxist-feminists.

"The building of socialism will begin only when we have achieved the complete equality of women and when we undertake the new work together with women who have been emancipated from that petty stultifying, unproductive work.... The chief thing is to get women to take part in socially productive labor"—Vladimir Lenin

In 1975, French Marxist-feminist Simone de Beauvoir, who worked for most of her life advancing her beliefs, told Betty Friedan in an interview, "No woman should be authorized to stay at home to raise her children. Society should be totally different. Women should not have that choice, precisely because if there is such a choice, too many women will make that one."[217] Fast forward to 2013 when Sharon Smith, author of *Women and Socialism: Essays on Women's Liberation*, wrote for *SocialistWorker.org* about the decades of work by Marxist-feminists like de Beauvoir: "This group of feminists has been developing and expanding the Marxist understanding of the role women play in reproducing the working class as a service to the capitalist system.... These feminists have not only played a key role in advancing Marxist theory on women's oppression, but they remind us that Marxism is a living, breathing theory that is still in the process of developing. And deepening Marxist and feminist theory means also deepening and expanding the potential for our future practice in combatting women's oppression."[218] This viewpoint is shared by others who wouldn't call themselves "Marxists," "socialists," or even "feminists." Jordan Weissmann—an *economist*—complains in a 2019 article for *Slate*: "Why did American women stop storming the job market? *Much of the fault lies with our archaic family policies.* Other countries took steps to ensure more mothers could work.... And by limiting the share of women who are able to work, we're limiting the size of our labor force. We're straitjacketing the economy."[219] (Emphasis added.)

# XIII. Rubble

"The family is ceasing to be necessary either to its members or to the nation"—Alexandra Kollontai, first People's Commissar for Social Welfare

In the landmark case *Perry v. Schwarzenegger*, the United States District Court for the Northern District of California defined marriage as "the state recognition and approval of a couple's choice to live with each other, to remain committed to one another and to form a household based on their own feelings about one another and to join in an economic partnership and support one another and any dependents." When the case went before the Supreme Court of the United States as *Hollingsworth v. Perry* in 2013, the Justice Department argued that children do not have the right to a mother and a father.[220] Building upon this, in 2016, a UN report prepared ahead of the 2016 UN Human Rights Council meeting said the family should be understood "in a wide sense" and that "There is no definition of the family under international human rights law."[221] Some "big thinkers" are taking the concept of marriage even further. Transhumanist Zoltan Istvan said in a recent article, "It's even possible that by not encouraging my daughter to be open to love [robots] in the future, I might be shortchanging her, which is the last thing a parent would ever want to do. Ultimately, I believe in loving my daughter, regardless how sophisticated technology becomes. If she chooses as an adult to marry anyone or *anything*—so long as she has rationally and deeply thought all of it through—then I want to support her choices. Even if in the future her spouse is not of human form."[222] (Emphasis added) Zoltan regularly appears as a commentator on television and writes for popular publications such as *Wired*, *Newsweek*, and *The Huffington Post*.

"The old type of family has had its day. The family is withering away not because it is being forcibly destroyed by the state, but because the family is ceasing to be a necessity."—Alexandra Kollontai

There is no shortage of articles and books proclaiming that the "old type of family" is dead, that we don't need it anymore, and that new models of "families" are just as good if not better than the "old type of family." For example, Emma Johnson, writing for *wealthysinglemommy.com* in 2018, tells her readers that "Co-parenting is the future, and the future is now.... Steel yourself not for friendship or even a sense of family. At least not yet. Instead, you open yourself to a relationship that you have not yet defined, but will explore. And everything is better."[223] The website *thenewfamily.com* touts their "award-winning blog project, 'I bet we can find 1,000 ways to be a family.'"[224] Bustle, a website targeting millennial women with an audience of 80 million readers, ran an article in 2017 that tells readers that there are at least seven alternatives to traditional marriage, including the "starter marriage," "parenting marriage," "living alone together marriage," and "open marriage."[225] In fact, a quick Google search for "alternatives to traditional marriage" returned about 18,000,000 results.

"[In Spain,] as far as possible every church and every monastery was destroyed. Every vestige of the Christian religion was eradicated.... the majority of its victims have been laymen of all conditions and classes.... masses of them are slain almost daily for no other offense than the fact that they are good Christians or at least opposed to atheistic Communism.... No man of good sense, nor any statesman conscious of his responsibility can fail to shudder at the thought that what is happening today in Spain may perhaps be repeated tomorrow in other civilized countries."—Pope Pius XI, Divini Redemptoris

The persecution of Christians in Spain in the 1930's was also taking place elsewhere. This persecution of Christians continued behind the Iron Curtain through the late 1980s and even after the dissolution of the Soviet Union. In total, an estimated 23,900,000 Christians of all denominations were killed by the Communist government of the Soviet Union between 1921 and 1980.[226] The brutal persecution of Christians at the hands of the Communists continues to this very day:

**27 April 2016:** "Government officials in China's coastal Zhejiang province have ordered the destruction of yet another church building as part of an ongoing campaign against so-called illegal buildings.... China Aid President Bof Fu previously told *The Christian Post* that the campaign reflects the Communist Party's concerns about the growing number of Christians in the country. 'The top leadership is increasingly worried about the rapid growth of Christian faith and their public presence, and their social influence,' Fu told *CP* back in February. 'It is a political fear for the Communist Party, as the number of Christians in the country far outnumber the members of the party,' he added. Christians protesting against persecution have found themselves arrested by Communist authorities, while standing up to forced church demolition has also proven deadly for others. Earlier in April, the wife of a church leader died after being buried alive by a demolition crew, after she and her husband tried to protest the destruction of their church in Zhumadian, Henan province." [227]

**11 June 2017:** "Violence broke out in Shanggiu in Henan province after 300 police officers and officials demolished the Shuangmiao Christian Church—which was under construction.... China Aid said: 'During the demolition, officials beat dozens of church members, pushing them to the ground and twisting their hands.' ... According to churchgoers Xi Jinping's Communist Party ordered the church to be destroyed after branding the building an 'illegal structure' ... Churches not sanctioned by the government have been put under surveillance with hundreds of Christians arrested for disturbing public order for offences [sic] such as holding bible study groups and displaying crucifixes outside their homes."[228]

**11 January 2018:** "The Chinese government this week demolished with explosives a Christian megachurch in its northern Shanxi province, prompting Christian fears of heightened persecution under the government's atheistic Communist regime. Golden Lampstand Church in Linfen, Shanxi was destroyed by the paramilitary People's Armed Police forces on Tuesday, who reportedly used excavators and dynamite to destroy the church, according to ChinaAid. The 50,000 strong church was originally built with 17 million Yuan (around $2.5 million) of congregation contributions."[229]

**26 October 2018:** "Chinese authorities demolished two Catholic pilgrimage sites dedicated to the Virgin Mary just weeks after the Vatican signed a deal with the Communist Party over the appointment of bishops. Reports and videos showing the demolition of the two sanctuaries became public Thursday, according to *AsiaNews*, the official press agency of the Pontifical Institute for Foreign Missions. The shrine of Our Lady of the Seven Sorrows in Dongergou (Shanxi) was apparently destroyed Thursday, while Our Lady of the Mountain, in Anlong (Guizhou) was destroyed this week."[230]

# XIII. Rubble

## FRANKFURT SCHOOL

"The power of the culture industry's ideology is such that conformity has replaced consciousness."—Theodor Adorno

A series of experiments performed by psychologist Solomon Asch in the 1950s showed that people are so swayed by popular opinion that they will choose an obviously wrong answer if it means conforming to what everyone else thinks. Decades of research since then have only reinforced this finding. Today, we are surrounded by cues to conform to a certain norm or standard. The media that we consume—television, movies, magazines, music, and social media—portray an idealized notion of life, and we are by our very nature driven to conform with what we perceive to be "normal," "accepted," and "popular." A recent UCLA experiment mapped brain activity in teens who were shown pictures in a controlled setting that mimicked social media. The experiment showed that the more "likes" something got, *regardless* of the quality of the content, the more likely it was for the teen to also "like" it. What's more, the experiment found that simply viewing images of illicit behavior such as drug and alcohol use *decreased* the activity in the part of the brain involved in rational thought. So the mere *exposure* to images of risky behavior decreased the ability of teens to think and realize that the behavior was even risky.[231]

"The majority principle ... is a new god ... a power of resistance to anything that does not conform."—Max Horkheimer

The culture wars that have divided society have now evolved to a point at which opposing sides engage in public shaming of people who do not conform to their point of view. Social media has been used to direct a flood of anger and ridicule toward family, friends, and total strangers alike. Terms like "hashtag campaigns," "doxxing," and "cancelling" have emerged to describe various techniques used by people who push for conformity to their way of thinking. Stories are everywhere about people who say or do one thing wrong in a moment of mental foolishness, then find themselves on the receiving end of everything from hate emails to death threats against their family members. As Todd Leopold wrote for CNN in 2015, "These days, it's not enough for someone who's screwed up to be rebuked. Even an apology and remorse are rarely enough. On social media—Twitter especially, with its global reach and lack of irony—that person must be destroyed."[232] This has led to job losses, school expulsions, marital strife, depression, and even suicide. The popularity of social media has given rise to people struggling to maintain an online persona that is the image of a "perfect" life seen by their followers.[233] Psychologists and sociologists who have studied social media have determined that there is little correlation between people's online lives and their real lives.[234]

"It is possible that mankind is on the threshold of a golden age; but, if so, it will be necessary first to slay the dragon that guards the door, and this dragon is religion."—Lord Bertrand Russell

In 1991, those in the United States who claimed no religious affiliation stood at about 7% of the population, which was about average going back several decades. By 2018 the number of those professing no religious affiliation—also called "nones"—had risen to just over 23%. In the meantime, those professing an affiliation to mainline Protestant Christianity—such as Lutherans, Methodists, Presbyterians, and Baptists—have seen a 62.5% decline in believers since 1982, now making up only around 11% of the US population.[235] This is due in part to the rise of militant atheists—whose god is science—and the active promotion of their message via popular media platforms. One of the most prominent militant atheists is Richard Dawkins, who was heavily influenced by the works of Lord Bertrand Russell. Dawkins published 14 books between 1976 and 2017, including the 2006 international bestseller *The God Delusion*. He has appeared in numerous documentaries and interviews, regularly writes for various magazines newspapers, and online publications, and won multiple awards including the *Los Angeles Times* Literary Prize for his 1986 book *The Blind Watchmaker*. In a 2002 TED talk, he encouraged those who "despise religion as much as I do" to "stop being polite, come out, and say so" in order to fight organized religion and its influence in society. According to the TED webpage where the video can be found, "This talk was presented at an official TED conference, and was featured by our editors on the home page."[236] To perpetuate and spread his ideas, Dawkins founded the Richard Dawkins Foundation for Reason and Science in 2006, and it has been actively participating in efforts to advance secularism in schools and politics. Dawkins is not alone. Other militant atheists such as Christopher Hitchens, Sam Harris, and Daniel Dennett, in addition to being bestselling authors, make frequent contributions to media outlets such as the *Washington Post, Huffington Post, Newsweek,* the *New York Times,* the *Los Angeles Times,* the *Boston Globe,* ABC News, NPR, *The Colbert Report, The Daily Show,* and countless others.

"If there is only One God then there is no choice, no option, no selection of reality." —Timothy Leary

While the percent of the population that professes no religious affiliation has increased, so has the number of people who claim to be "spiritual but not religious." Many people have decided to cast off the dogmas of organized religion, and do what feels right to them. Each person of the spiritual but not religious crowd comes up with his own concoction of practices to drive his beliefs. These may include rocks and crystals, tarot cards, bits of Christianity, Judaism, Hinduism, Buddhism, and Islam, astrology, cultural religious practices, and more. They all believe in some sort of higher power, but whether it is a singular God, a collection of gods and goddesses, or just "the forces of the universe" depends on who you ask. And if you have a different view on things, that's fine with them too. To someone who is spiritual but not religious, organized religion is frequently perceived as too dogmatic, requires too much obedience, has empty rituals, has too much shame and guilt, and talks too much about sin and Hell. Author, speaker, and meditation teacher Giovanni Dienstmann says on his website, "Spirituality says every person has a unique path.... Since the time of the European Enlightenment in the 17th century, the role and dominion of religion seem to be steadily diminishing (at least in the Western world). Since we entered the so-called 'age of reason,' with the ability of science to explain and transform reality around us constantly increasing, and the general level of education also rising for everyone, people feel less drawn to seek organized religion as a tool for explaining the world and creating well-being."[237] Self-proclaimed "seeker and researcher of spiritual wisdom" D. Patrick Miller explains, "instead of attempting to obey and please 'God the Father' according to religious rules set down in the Bible or given by one's church, the spiritual aspirant strives to become Godlike in his or her attitudes and behaviors."[238] As of 2017, a Pew Research poll showed that 27% of Americans consider themselves "spiritual but not religious."[239]

"Man wants to be his own master, and alone
— always and exclusively—
to determine everything that concerns him.

"Yet in this way he lives in opposition to the truth,
in opposition to the Creator Spirit."

POPE BENEDICT XVI, 2008

# EPILOGUE

SATAN'S attack on marriage, on the Domestic Church, is his way of attacking Christ's Church, which saves souls from eternal damnation. When Domestic Churches fail and fall to temptation and sin, what is the result? Fewer marriages. Fewer children, which means fewer people who enter the religious life. Fewer people following the laws of God. More children being raised in households where God's laws are not followed, where the errors of modernism, rationalism, idolatry, schism, apostasy, and heresies are handed down from generation to generation. The dwindling few who do enter religious life may then carry these aberrations with them into Christ's Church. This is the story of Satan's rebellious war against the Most High. It all started with marriage, and continues to be rooted in marriage.

What was once merely a battle of Satan against God turned into a battle of faith, religion, politics, and culture. In the world today, every Domestic Church, every family, is on the front lines of that battle, fighting against what St. Paul described in his letter to the Galatians. He warned that those who engage in "immorality, impurity, licentiousness, idolatry, sorcery, hatreds, rivalry, jealousy, outbursts of fury, acts of selfishness, dissensions, factions, occasions of envy, drinking bouts, orgies, and the like"[240] would not inherit the kingdom of God.

Throughout the history of the Old Testament, after Original Sin, we see a pattern repeat:

1. God gives us His rules clearly, in easy to understand fashion.

2. We start to break God's rules, so He sends a prophet to warn us to repent and mend our ways.

3. Those who fail to turn back to God are chastised.

4. When we have suffered greatly at the hands of the godless, God sends someone to lead us back to Him.

5. When we turn back to God, He blesses us abundantly.

Once more, we see this pattern in action: Our Lady of Good Success warned us, we didn't listen, and the corruption of Lisbon led to its chastisement and virtual destruction. The once-Catholic people of Portugal were then ruled by the godless Masonic sects, until Our Lady of Fatima came. When the people returned to their faith, God blessed them and protected them from the ravages of World War II. Our Lady of Fatima also issued a warning for the whole world, and we haven't listened. So today, because of God's justice, all who did not heed the message of Fatima are undergoing chastisement as our Domestic Churches fall apart one by one, and our society at large is falling apart along with them.

The world today is the world Satan has worked to achieve since he dared to desire to set his throne above the Most High. It is a world where we are encouraged to create an idol to worship *of ourselves*, rather than seek to be submissive to the promptings of the Holy Spirit within us and the transcendent God who exists outside of us. It is a world where we are each encouraged to create an idol that makes each of *us* feel in control, that makes each of *us* masters of our own lives, that gives each of *us* the power to decide what is right and moral and true. It is a world that destroys our relationship with God through the Holy Spirit and replaces Him with idols of ourselves, idols created by our own hands and minds.

The ivy of misperception did its work destroying Domestic Churches by driving people to create an "Idol of Self." It is an idol that not only exists within each one of us, but its growth and development has been—and continues to be—encouraged by all those who serve only their *own* Idols of Self. This Idol of Self, this false god of flawed human reason and misperception, is the false god of William of Ockham. It is the false god of Martin Luther. It is the false god of Giordano Bruno, Freemasons, Socialists, and Communists. It is the false god of Lord Bertrand Russell, Timothy Leary, Marxist-feminists, and atheists.

The Idol of Self is a false god that worships itself and its own beauty. It is a false god that looks inward, instead of outward, where "following your heart" means to serve yourself first. Being encouraged to serve this Idol of Self has led to the ruination of countless marriages, the damaging of generations of children, and the eternal damnation of an incalculable number of souls. The Idol of Self knows that God's truth will destroy it, so it builds walls to protect itself, making it difficult and sometimes impossible to accept God's truth. The Idol of Self tells us God's truth is actually a lie, that surely if we eat of the fruit of the tree, we will not die. Most of all, the Idol of Self is a rebellious creature shouting, "I will not serve!" This was never God's desire for us. This was never Christ's desire for His Church.

## KILLING THE IDOL OF SELF
The Idol of Self is always there inside each one of us, wanting attention. It draws our eyes down, away from the light, away from Heaven, away from God. For some, the Idol of Self is a creature of pride. For others, it is a creature of vanity or sensuality. The Idol of Self seeks out earthly substitutes for God: honor, power, wealth, and pleasure. It is always hungry, prowling around like a roaring lion, seeking to devour the soul with fruitless works of darkness. No matter how much earthly happiness it is fed, it always growls for more. Our rebellion against God comes down to violating the 1st Commandment: we either choose to worship the living and eternal God, or we choose to worship the Idol of Self.

Marriages were designed by God to help each of us and our children get to Heaven. Husbands and wives have a duty to live as children of light, to help each other identify fruitless works of darkness, and to lead their children to the light. For the sake of our marriages, our eternal souls, and the eternal souls of our children, we must fight against Satan and the distorted perceptions of reality he presents us. We must endeavor to search for what *is* true, not what we *perceive* to be true. We must work to restore within us the right order of reason over over emotion. We must be resolved to be obedient to God as Christ was obedient to God.

*We must end our rebellion.*

And ending the rebellion starts when we resolve to destroy our Idols of Self and undertake the labors necessary to build, protect, and defend the Domestic Church.

"Return, O Israelites,
to him whom you have utterly deserted.
On that day each one of you shall
reject his idols of silver and gold,
which your hands have made."

ISAIAH 31:6-7

# ENDNOTES

# Endnotes

1. Lara Bazelon, "Divorce Can Be An Act Of Radical Self-Love", *New York Times*. Sept. 30, 2021. https://www.nytimes.com/2021/09/30/opinion/divorce-children.html. Accessed Nov. 18, 2021.

2. Robert Samuelson, "Single Parenthood And Poverty, The Undeniable Connection", *Investor's Business Daily*. Mar. 18, 2018. https://www.investors.com/politics/columnists/single-parenthood-and-poverty-the-undeniable-connection/. Accessed Aug. 23, 2020.

3. W. Bradford Wilcox. "The Kids Are Not Really Alright", *Slate*. Jul. 20, 2012. https://slate.com/human-interest/2012/07/single-motherhood-worse-for-children.html. Accessed Aug. 23, 2020.

4. Jennie Brand, Ravaris Moore, Xi Song, and Yu Xie. "Why Does Parental Divorce Lower Children's Educational Attainment? A Causal Mediation Analysis", *Sociological Science* 6 (2019): 264-292. doi:10.15195/v6.a11.

5. Apocalypse 4:8,11

6. Genesis 2:24 RSVCE

7. Genesis 2:7

8. Genesis 2:15-20

9. Rev. Francis Spirago, and Rt. Rev. Msgr. Anthony N. Fuerst, S.T.D. *The Catechism Explained*. Trans. Rev. Richard Frederick Clarke S.J. (New York: Benzinger Brothers, 1961), 63.

10. Genesis 2:20-24

11. Genesis 1:28

12. Genesis 3:1-6

13. Wisdom 2:24

14. Aquinas, ST II-II. Q163

15. Aquinas, ST II-II. Q43

16. Spirago. *The Catechism Explained*. 63.

17. *Catechism of the Catholic Church*; (New York: Doubleday, 1997), 391

18. Spirago. *The Catechism Explained*. 65.

19. Genesis 3:16

20. Genesis 3:16-19

21. Genesis 3:12

22. Msgr. Charles Pope, "Why is the First Sin called the 'Sin of Adam' not the 'Sin of Adam and Eve?'" *Community in Mission* (blog) Aug. 30, 2010. https://blog.adw.org/2010/08/why-is-the-first-sin-called-the-sin-of-adam-not-the-sin-of-adam-and-eve. Accessed Apr. 2, 2019

23. Luke 1:28 (Douay-Rheims 1899 American Edition).

24. Stephen Beale, "What Do We Mean By Full Of Grace?" *Catholic Exchange* Jul. 28, 2014. https://catholicexchange.com/mean-full-grace. Accessed May 10, 2019

25. II Samuel 6:9

26. Luke 1:43

27. Exodus 40:34

28. Luke 1:35

29. John 1:14

30. John 1:14 30. (New American Bible Revised Edition study notes. Wichita: Devore & Sons, Inc. 2011)

31. Luke 1:38 (Douay-Rheims 1899 American Edition)

32. Mike Aquilina. *A Year With the Church Fathers: Patristic Wisdom for Daily Living*. (Charlotte: St. Benedict Press, 2010), 28.

33. *The New Confraternity Edition Revised Baltimore Catechism and Mass No. 3*, 4th ed. 95.

34. John 6:53

35. John 17:20-23

36. Spirago. *The Catechism Explained*. 113, 115

37. St. John Paul II, "*St. Michael Protects and Defends the Church, Visit to the Shrine of St. Michael on May 24, 1987 at Monte Gargano*", translation by *Opus Sanctorum Angelorum*. https://opusangelorum.org/catechesis-popes. Accessed 11/18/2021. Original https://w2.vatican.va/content/john-paul-ii/it/speeches/1987/may/documents/hf_jp-ii_spe_19870524_monte-sant-angelo.html. Accessed March 24, 2019.

38. Preserved Smith Ph.D. *The Life and Letters of Martin Luther*. (London: John Murray, 1911), 12.

39. Ken Hensley. "Luther: The Rest of the Story, Part II: The Road to Wittenberg", *Coming Home Network*, May 30, 2018. https://chnetwork.org/2018/05/30/luther-the-rest-of-the-story-part-ii-the-road-to-wittenberg. Accessed Dec. 10, 2019

40. Roland H. Bainton. *Here I Stand - A Life of Martin Luther*. (New York: Abingdon-Cokesbury Press, 1950), 65.

41. James Kittelson. *Luther The Reformer*. (Minneapolis: Augsburg Fortress Publishing House, 1986), 79.

42. Ken Hensley. "Luther: The Rest of the Story, Part II: The Road to Wittenberg"

43. Preserved Smith Ph.D. *The Life and Letters of Martin Luther*. 12.

44. Ken Hensley. "Luther: The Rest of the Story, Part II: The Road to Wittenberg"

45. David Armstrong. "William of Ockham, Nominalism, Luther, & Early Protestant Thought", *Patheos*. Oct. 10, 2017 https://www.patheos.com/blogs/davearmstrong/2017/10/william-ockham-nominalism-luther-early-protestant-thought.html. Accessed Dec. 6, 2019

46. Ibid.

47. Preserved Smith Ph.D. *The Life and Letters of Martin Luther*. 17.

48. Preserved Smith Ph.D. *The Life and Letters of Martin Luther*. 19.

49. Ken Hensley. "Luther: The Rest of the Story, Part II: The Road to Wittenberg"

50. Hilaire Belloc. "The Great Heresies", *EWTN* https://www.ewtn.com/catholicism/library/great-heresies-3103. Accessed Mar. 11, 2019.

51. The Very Rev. M. J. Lagrange, O.P. "Luther on the Eve of His Revolt" *EWTN*. Nov. 24, 1917 https://www.ewtn.com/catholicism/library/luther-on-the-eve-of-his-revolt-10326. Accessed Dec. 6, 2019.

52. Dr. Ludwig Pastor. *The History of the Popes from the Close of the Middle Ages, Volume VII* (London: Kegan Paul, Trench, Trubner & Co, Ltd, 1908), 366.

53. St. Augustine of Hippo. "Of the Morals of the Catholic Church" *New Advent*. 388 A.D. http://www.newadvent.org/fathers/1401.htm Accessed Apr. 11, 2019.

54. Martin Luther. "The Babylonian Captivity of the Church", 1520. Trans. A. T. W. Steinhäuser (1915), revised by Frederick C. Ahrens and Abdel Ross Wentz http://www.onthewing.org/user/Luther%20-%20Babylonian%20Captivity.pdf Accessed Apr. 10, 2019.

55. Galusha Anderson & Edgar Johnson Goodspeed. *Ancient Sermons for Modern Times* (New York: The Pilgrim Press, 1904), 136-141.

56. Roland H. Bainton. *Here I Stand - A Life of Martin Luther*. 189.

57. Rt. Rev. Mons. Patrick F. O'Hare. *The Facts About Luther* (New York: Frederick Pustet & Co., 1916), 207-209.

58. John L. Stoddard *Rebuilding a Lost Faith by an American Agnostic* (New York: P.J. Kenedy and Sons, 1922), 101-102.

59. Rt. Rev. Mons. Patrick F. O'Hare. *The Facts About Luther*. 206.

60. Hilaire Belloc. "The Great Heresies"

61. Jules Michelet. *The Life of Martin Luther Gathered from His Own Writings*, (New York: A.A. Kelley, 1858), 268-269

62. Stephen Beale. "Just How Many Protestant Denominations Are There?" *National Catholic Register* Oct. 31, 2017 http://www.ncregister.com/blog/sbeale/just-how-many-protestant-denominations-are-there. Accessed May 8, 2019.

63. Mark 3:25

64. References to "queen mother" in the NABRE translation: 1 Kings 15:13; II Kings 10:13; II Chronicles 15:16; Jeremiah 13:18 & 29:2

65. John 19:26-27

66. Jane Stannus. "The remarkable story behind Our Lady's prophecies from Ecuador", *The Catholic Herald* Feb. 2, 2019. https://catholicherald.co.uk/the-remarkable-story-behind-our-ladys-prophecies-from-ecuador. Accessed Nov. 18, 2021.

67. Sister Mary Agatha, CMRI. "Our Lady of Good Success and the Message of Fatima", *The Reign of Mary*, Issue 121, 2005. http://www.cmri.org/05-our-lady-of-good-success.shtml. Accessed May 8, 2019.

68. Steve Skojec. "400 Years Ago, Our Lady Sent Us A Message From Ecuador" *1 Peter 5* Jul. 6, 2015. https://onepeterfive.com/400-years-ago-our-lady-sent-us-a-message-from-ecuador. Accessed May 14, 2019.

69. "Marian Apparitions Deemed 'Worthy of Belief'", *Fish Eaters*. https://www.fisheaters.com/apparitions.html#success. Accessed May 9, 2019.

70. Monsignor Luis E. Cadena y Almeida *A Spanish Mystic in Quito: Sor Mariana de Jesus Torres*. (New York: The Foundation for a Christian Civilization, 1990), 97-99.

71. Mark Molesky. *This Gulf of Fire*. (New York: Vintage Books, 2015), 55.

72. Ibid. 13.

73. Clara Vasconcelos, Joana Torres, Joana Costa. "What happens to the boats? The 1755 Lisbon earthquake and Portuguese tsunami literacy", *GeoScienceWorld* June 1, 2017. https://pubs.geoscienceworld.org/gsa/geosphere/article-standard/13/3/723/208045/what-happens-to-the-boats-the-1755-lisbon. Accessed May 15, 2019.

74. John 15:1-6

75. Matthew 28:19-20

76. John 14:6 (Douay-Rheims 1899 American Edition)

77. Laura Miller. "The heretic", *Salon*. Aug. 25, 2008. https://www.salon.com/2008/08/25/bruno_2. Accessed Apr. 25, 2019.

78. Ibid.

79. Ibid.

80. Joan Acocella. "The Forbidden World", *New Yorker* Aug. 18, 2008. https://www.newyorker.com/magazine/2008/08/25/the-forbidden-world. Accessed Apr. 25, 2019.

81. Ibid.

82. Marc Kaufman. "Cosmic Crusader", *Washington Post*. Aug. 10, 2008. http://www.washingtonpost.com/wp-dyn/content/article/2008/08/07/AR2008080702384.html. Accessed Apr. 25, 2019.

83. Joan Acocella. "The Forbidden World".

84. Laura Miller. "The heretic".

85. Kevin Symonds. *Pope Leo XIII and the Prayer to St. Michael*, (Boonville: Preserving Christian Publications, 2015), 132.

86. Ibid. 103.

87. Msgr. George F. Dillon. *Grand Orient Freemasonry Unmasked as the Secret Power Behind Communism*. (London: Britons Publishing Company, 1950), 89-90, 92.

88. Ibid. 106-108.

89. Ibid. 103-104.

90. Sacred Congregation for the Doctrine of the Faith *Quaesitum Est: Declaration on Masonic Associations* Nov. 26, 1983 https://www.vatican.va/roman_curia/congregations/cfaith/documents/rc_con_cfaith_doc_19831126_declaration-masonic_en.html. Accessed Dec. 21, 2021.

91. Brother Francis M. Kalvelage, FI, editor. *Kolbe, Saint of the Immaculata*. (New Bedford: Franciscans of the Immaculate, 2001), 32.

92. Pope Benedict XV. *Sacra Propoediem* https://www.vatican.va/content/benedict-xv/en/encyclicals/documents/hf_ben-xv_enc_06011921_sacra-propediem.html. Accessed 11/18/2021.

93. Ed Condon. "The real reason Catholics cannot be Freemasons", *Catholic Herald*. Aug. 10, 2017. https://catholicherald.co.uk/the-real-reason-catholics-cant-be-freemasons. Accessed Nov. 18, 2021.

94. Ibid.

95. Paula Findlen. "A Hungry Mind: Giordano Bruno, Philosopher and Heretic", *The Nation*. Sept. 29, 2008 https://www.thenation.com/article/hungry-mind-giordano-bruno-philosopher-and-heretic. Accessed April 25, 2019.

96. Joan Acocella. "The Forbidden World".

97. Pope Benedict XVI, Joseph Ratzinger. *In the Beginning: A Catholic Understanding of the Story of Creation and the Fall*. 1986. Trans. by Boniface Ramsey O.P. (Grand Rapids: William B. Eerdmans Publishing Company, 1995), 83.

98. Ibid. 83-84.

99. Pope Leo XIII. *Dall'alto Dell'apostolico Seggio—Encyclical Of Pope Leo XIII On Freemasonry In Italy*. Oct. 15, 1890. http://w2.vatican.va/content/leo-xiii/en/encyclicals/documents/hf_l-xiii_enc_18901015_apostolico-seggio.html. Accessed Apr. 29, 2019.

100. Pope Pius IX. *Qui Pluribus (On Faith And Religion)*. Nov. 9, 1846 *Papal Encyclicals Online*. https://www.papalencyclicals.net/Pius09/p9quiplu.htm. Accessed Dec. 21, 2021.

101. Rose L. Martin. *Fabian Freeway: The High Road to Socialism in the U.S.A.* (Belmont: Western Islands, 1966), 12.

102. Rose L. Martin. *Fabian Freeway*. 12.

103. Rose L. Martin. *Fabian Freeway*. 55.

104. George Bernard Shaw. "What Socialism Is, Fabian Tract #13", *The Fabian Society*. (London: 1890), https://digital.library.lse.ac.uk/objects/lse:wav875fun. Accessed May 2, 2019.

105. Rose L. Martin. *Fabian Freeway*. 16.

106. Eduard Bernstein. "My Years of Exile, Chapter X, The socialist intellectuals in England", *Marxists.org*. https://www.marxists.org/reference/archive/bernstein/works/1915/exile/ch10.htm. Accessed May 2, 2019.

107. Sister Mary Margaret McCarran, Ph.D. *Fabianism in the Political Life of Britain 1919-1931*, 2nd ed. (Chicago: The Heritage Foundation, 1954), 26.

108. Rose L. Martin. *Fabian Freeway*. 57.

109. Reverend Stewart D. Headlam. "Christian Socialism", *The Fabian Society*. (London: 1892), https://digital.library.lse.ac.uk/objects/lse:xoj874buh. Accessed May 2, 2019.

110. John 9:1-3

111. John 9:39

112. Reverend Percy Dearmer. "Socialism and Christianity", *The Fabian Society*. (London: 1907), https://digital.library.lse.ac.uk/objects/lse:fad722dem. Accessed May 2, 2019.

113. Pope Pius IX. *Nostis Et Nobiscum (On the Church in the Pontifical States)*. Dec. 8, 1849. *Papal Encyclicals Online*. http://www.papalencyclicals.net/Pius09/p9nostis.htm. Accessed March 16, 2019.

114. Pope Leo XIII. *Quod Apostolici Muneris (On Socialism)*. Dec. 28, 1878. https://w2.vatican.va/content/leo-xiii/en/encyclicals/documents/hf_l-xiii_enc_28121878_quod-apostolici-muneris.html. Accessed March 16, 2019.

115. Monsignor John A. Ryan. "A living Wage: Its Ethical and Economic Aspects", (New York: The Macmillan Company, 1912). viii.

116. Rose L. Martin. *Fabian Freeway*. 214.

117. Rose L. Martin. *Fabian Freeway*. 34.

118. Richard Weikart. "Marx, Engels, and the Abolition of the Family", *History of European Ideas, Vol. 18, No. 5* (Great Britain: Elsevier Science Ltd., 1994) 658.

119. Rose L. Martin. *Fabian Freeway*. 121.

120. Vladimir Ilyich Lenin. "Friedrich Engels", *Marxists.org*. 1895. https://www.marxists.org/archive/lenin/works/1895/misc/engels-bio.htm. Accessed March 22, 2019.

121. Pope Pius IX. *Qui Pluribus (On Faith And Religion)*.

122. Pope Leo XIII. *Rerum Novarum (On Capital And Labor)*. May 15, 1891. https://w2.vatican.va/content/leo-xiii/en/encyclicals/documents/hf_l-xiii_enc_15051891_rerum-novarum.html. Accessed Mar. 25, 2019.

123. Rose L. Martin. *Fabian Freeway*. 56

124. Matt Archbold "'Taken Into the Arms of Mary'—When Joseph Stalin's Daughter Became Catholic", *National Catholic Register*. Aug. 28, 2019. https://www.ncregister.com/blog/when-joseph-stalin-s-daughter-became-catholic. Accessed Nov. 18, 2021.

125. "Soviet persecution of church mourned", *The Washington Times*. Nov. 7, 2004. https://www.washingtontimes.com/news/2004/nov/7/20041107-110921-8459r. Accessed May 7, 2019.

126. Jonathan Luxmoore. "Time to recall Christian martyrs to communism, says Russian catholic church", *The Tablet*. Aug 15, 2017. https://www.thetablet.co.uk/news/7631/time-to-recall-christian-martyrs-to-communism-says-russian-catholic-church. Accessed May 7, 2019.

127. "Persecution of Christians in the Soviet Union", *Wikipedia*. https://en.wikipedia.org/wiki/Persecution_of_Christians_in_the_Soviet_Union. Accessed May 7, 2019.

128. "League of Militant Atheists", *Wikipedia* https://en.wikipedia.org/wiki/League_of_Militant_Atheists. Accessed March 25, 2019.

129. Pope Pius XI. *Divini Redemptoris (On Atheistic Communism)*. https://www.vatican.va/content/pius-xi/en/encyclicals/documents/hf_p-xi_enc_19370319_divini-redemptoris.html. Accessed Nov. 18, 2021.

130. Clara Zetkin. "Lenin on the Women's Question", *Marxists.org*. https://www.marxists.org/archive/zetkin/1920/lenin/zetkin1.htm. Accessed March 22, 2019.

131. Fr. Benedict Kiely. "The Vatican's Deal With The Dragon", *The American Conservative*. Sept. 23, 2020. https://www.theamericanconservative.com/articles/the-vaticans-deal-with-the-dragon. Accessed Sept. 24, 2020.

132. Valbona Bezati. "How Albania Became the World's First Atheist Country", *Balkan Transitional Justice*. Aug. 28, 2019. https://balkaninsight.com/2019/08/28/how-albania-became-the-worlds-first-atheist-country. Accessed Sept. 24, 2020.

133. Robert Royal. "Albania: The First Atheist State", *Catholic Education Resource Center*. 2000. https://www.catholiceducation.org/en/controversy/persecution/albania-the-first-atheist-state.html. Accessed 10/19/2020

134. Fr. Benedict Kiely. "Resurrection in Albania", *First Things*. Jul. 23, 2019. https://www.firstthings.com/web-exclusives/2019/07/resurrection-in-albania. Accessed Sept. 24, 2019.

135. Pope Pius XII. "Decree against communism", *Montfort Associação Cultural*. 1949. http://www.montfort.org.br/eng/documentos/decretos/anticomunismo. Accessed March 25, 2019.

136. Thomas J. Craughwell. "How the Church Was Destroyed in Shanghai", *National Catholic Register*. May 8, 2012. https://www.ncregister.com/daily-news/how-the-church-was-destroyed-in-shanghai. Accessed May 8, 2019.

137. Ibid.

138. Elise Harris. "'Miracle of the sun' broke darkness of Portugal's atheist regimes", *Catholic News Agency*. Oct. 12, 2017. https://www.catholicnewsagency.com/news/miracle-of-the-sun-broke-darkness-of-portugals-atheist-regimes-28148. Accessed May 15, 2019.

139. Fr. Louis Kondor, SVD, Editor. *Fatima in Lucia's Own Words*, 14th ed. Trans. Dominican Nuns of Perpetual Rosary. (Fatima: Secretariado Dos Pastorinhos, 2004), 178.

140. Father Antonio Maria Martins, S.J. *Documents on Fatima & the Memoirs of Sister Lucia*. (Alexandria: Fatima Family Apostolate, 1992), 125-126.

141. Ibid. 132.

142. "Circumstances and Dialogue of the 1917 Apparitions", *Fatima Archive*. https://fatima.org/about/fatima-the-facts/circumstances-and-dialogue-of-the-1917-apparitions. Accessed Nov. 18, 2021.

143. Ibid.

144. Deacon Nick Donnelly. "Our Lady Of Fatima And The Battle With Freemasonry, Part 1", *Church Militant*. Feb. 25, 2017. https://www.churchmilitant.com/news/article/our-lady-of-fatima-and-the-battle-with-freemasonry-part. Accessed Apr. 30, 2019.

145. Father Antonio Maria Martins, S.J. *Documents on Fatima & the Memoirs of Sister Lucia*. 169.

146. Alice Reis Israel. "Witness to the Miracle of the Sun—Our Lady's Blue Army", *World Apostolate of Fatima, USA*. Oct 10, 2017. https://www.bluearmy.com/witness-to-the-miracle-of-the-sun. Accessed May 22, 2019.

147. Ibid.

148. "Circumstances and Dialogue of the 1917 Apparitions"

149. John Nahrgang. "A translation of Avelino de Almeida's firsthand account of the Miracle of the Sun, published on October 15th, 1917, in O Século's daily edition", *World Apostolate of Fatima, USA*. https://www.bluearmy.com/wp-content/uploads/2016/11/Episode-8_Newspaper-reports-from-Fatima-1917.pdf 12. Accessed May 16, 2019.

150. "Silencing Of The Messengers: Father Fuentes (1959 – 1965)", *The Fatima Center* https://fatima.org/about/fatima-opposed/silencing-of-the-messengers-father-fuentes-1959-1965. Accessed May 16, 2019.

151. Deacon Nick Donnelly. "Our Lady Of Fatima And The Battle With Freemasonry, Part 1"

152. Grant M. Dahl. "Buchanan: 'Cultural Marxism' Has Succeeded Where Marx and Lenin Failed", *CNS News*. Oct. 19, 2011. https://www.cnsnews.com/blog/grant-m-dahl/buchanan-cultural-marxism-has-succeeded-where-marx-and-lenin-failed. Accessed May 20, 2019.

153. Vladimir I. Lenin. "The New Economic Policy: And The Tasks Of The Political Education Departments", *Marxists.org*. Oct. 17, 1921 https://www.marxists.org/archive/lenin/works/1921/oct/17.htm. Accessed May 20, 2019.

154. Steven Merritt Miner. "A Revolution Doomed From the Start", March 9, 1997. *New York Times*. https://archive.nytimes.com/

# Endnotes

www.nytimes.com/books/97/03/09/reviews/970309.09minert.html. Accessed May 20, 2019.

155. Gary DeMar. "Cultural Marxism's Long Ideological History Had One Major Goal The American Vision", *American Vision.* May 2, 2019. https://americanvision.org/19443/cultural-marxisms-long-ideological-history-had-one-major-goal. Accessed May 18, 2019.

156. Fr. James Thornton. "Gramsci's Grand Plan", *New American.* Jul. 5, 1999. https://www.thenewamerican.com/culture/history/item/15545-gramscis-grand-plan. Accessed May 18, 2019.

157. Arnaud de Lassus. "The Frankfurt School: Cultural Revolution", *Angelus Online.* Jul. 2006. http://www.angelusonline.org/index.php?section=articles&subsection=show_article&article_id=2514. Accessed May 18, 2019.

158. Timothy Matthews. "The Frankfurt School: Conspiracy to Corrupt", *Catholic Insight.* Mar. 2009. https://www.scribd.com/document/271281403/The-Frankfurt-School-Timothy-Matthews. 5. Accessed May 17, 2019.

159. Ibid. 4.

160. Arnaud de Lassus. "The Frankfurt School: Cultural Revolution".

161. Lord Bertrand Russell. *The Impact of Science on Society.* (New York: AMS Press, 1953) 30. https://archive.org/details/TheImpactOfScienceOnSociety-B.Russell. Accessed May 23, 2019.

162. Ibid. 50.

163. Lord Bertrand Russell. *The Scientific Outlook.* (London: George Allen & Unwin Ltd, 1931), 200.

164. David J. Peterson. "Bertrand Russell: Prophet of the New World Order", *Catholic Culture.* https://www.catholicculture.org/culture/library/view.cfm?recnum=2952. Accessed May 19, 2019.

165. Timothy Matthews. "The Frankfurt School: Conspiracy to Corrupt", 7.

166. "The Frankfurt School and 'Critical Theory'", *Marxists.org.* https://www.marxists.org/subject/frankfurt-school. Accessed 5/28/2019

167. "Encyclopedia of Marxism: Glossary of People: Re", *Marxists.org.* https://www.marxists.org/glossary/people/r/e.htm#reich-wilhelm. Accessed May 28, 2019.

168. Herbert Marcuse. *Eros and Civilization: A Philosophical Inquiry into Freud.* (Boston: Beacon Press, 1974), xi, xxv.

169. Wilhelm Reich. *The Sexual Revolution.* (New York: Orgone Institute Press, 1945), 73.

170. Ibid. 71.

171. Ibid. 258.

172. "The Russian Effort to Abolish Marriage", *The Atlantic.* Jul. 1926. https://www.theatlantic.com/magazine/archive/1926/07/the-russian-effort-to-abolish-marriage/306295. Accessed May 30, 2019.

173. Stephen Walford. "Our Lady of Civitavecchia 25 Years On", *La Stampa.* Aug. 25, 2020. https://www.lastampa.it/vatican-insider/en/2020/08/25/news/our-lady-of-civitavecchia-25-years-on-1.39230135. Accessed Jan. 6, 2021

174. Ibid.

175. "Fatima visionary predicted 'final battle' would be over marriage, family", *Catholic News Agency.* Dec. 31, 2016 https://www.catholicnewsagency.com/news/fatima-visionary-predicted-final-battle-would-be-over-marriage-family-17760. Accessed Nov. 28, 2018.

176. Dorothy Cummings McLean. "For sale on Etsy: nine 'consecrated' communion hosts 'for abuse'", *LifeSiteNews.* May 8, 2019. https://www.lifesitenews.com/news/for-sale-on-etsy-nine-consecrated-communion-hosts-for-abuse. Accessed Jun. 23, 2019.

177. Dorothy Cummings McLean. "Blessed Sacrament and tabernacle stolen from North Carolina Catholic Church", *LifeSiteNews.* Jun. 22, 2020. https://www.lifesitenews.com/news/blessed-sacrament-and-tabernacle-stolen-from-north-carolina-catholic-church. Accessed Jun. 23, 2019.

178. Nathan Cherry. "Marriage Redefinition is Just the Beginning", *Illinois Family Institute.* Mar. 27, 2013. https://illinoisfamily.org/homosexuality/marriage-redefinition-is-just-the-beginning. Accessed Aug. 26, 2020.

179. Julia Taliesin. "Somerville recognizes polyamorous domestic partnerships", *WickedLocal.* Jul. 1, 2020. https://somerville.wickedlocal.com/news/20200701/somerville-recognizes-polyamorous-domestic-partnerships. Accessed Aug. 26, 2020.

180. Aubrey Pound. "Teen Vogue encourages 13-year-olds to make child porn through sexting", *LifeSiteNews.* Mar. 26, 2020. LifeSiteNews.com https://www.lifesitenews.com/opinion/teen-vogue-encourages-13-year-olds-to-make-child-porn-through-sexting. Accessed Apr. 29, 2020.

181. Maryanne White. "Letter to the Editor: The legging problem", *The Observer.* Mar. 25, 2019. https://ndsmcobserver.com/2019/03/the-legging-problem. Accessed Aug. 26, 2020.

182. "Student Population at University of Notre Dame (ND)", *College Tuition Compare.* https://www.collegetuitioncompare.com/edu/152080/university-of-notre-dame/enrollment/#gender-block. Accessed Aug. 26, 2020.

183. Jeremy Bauer-Wolf. "The Legging Problem", *Inside Higher Ed.* Apr. 1, 2019. https://www.insidehighered.com/news/2019/04/01/letter-criticizing-notre-dame-women-wearing-leggings-prompts-campus-debate. Accessed Aug. 26, 2020.

184. Matt Villano. "All in: Gambling options proliferate across USA" *USAToday.* Jan. 26, 2013. https://www.usatoday.com/story/travel/destinations/2013/01/24/gambling-options-casinos-proliferate-across-usa/1861835. Accessed Jun.11, 2019.

185. Andrew Selsky. "Oregon, awash in marijuana, takes steps to curb production", *APNews.* May 31, 2019. https://www.apnews.com/eaea113eee94421789b24fcf047f6bae. Accessed May 31, 2019.

186. Jesse McKinley. "Could Prostitution Be the Next Vice to Be Decriminalized?", *New York Times.* May 31, 2019. https://www.nytimes.com/2019/05/31/nyregion/presidential-candidates-prostitution.html. Accessed May 31, 2019.

187. "Can You Guess 2018's Most-Viewed Porn Categories On The Largest XXX Site?", *Fight the New Drug.* Jul. 9, 2019. https://

fightthenewdrug.org/pornhub-visitors-in-2018-and-review-of-top-searches. Accessed Jul. 5, 2019.

188. Brother Francis M. Kalvelage, FI, editor. *Kolbe, Saint of the Immaculata*. 40.

189. "Catholic Church Attendance Drops", *Catholic League*. Apr. 9, 2018. https://www.catholicleague.org/catholic-church-attendance-drops. Accessed Apr. 5, 2019.

190. "Mass attendance in U.S. down in recent years, Gallup poll finds", *Catholic News Agency*. Apr. 11, 2018. https://cruxnow.com/church-in-the-usa/2018/04/11/mass-attendance-in-us-down-in-recent-years-gallup-poll-finds. Accessed Apr. 5, 2019.

191. Valerie Bauman. "Is America becoming Godless? The number of people who have no religion has risen 266 per cent—one third of the population—in three decades", *Daily Mail*. Apr. 6, 2019. https://www.dailymail.co.uk/news/article-6886705/Is-America-Godless-number-people-no-religion-rose-266-three-decades.html. Accessed Apr. 6, 2019.

192. Marcia Segelstein. "How to Protect Your Kids from Pornography" *National Catholic Register*. Apr. 24, 2019. https://www.ncregister.com/blog/how-to-protect-your-kids-from-pornography. Accessed Apr. 29, 2019.

193. "Massachusetts Family Institute—Pornography", *Massachusetts Family Institute*. https://www.mafamily.org/internet-safety. Accessed Apr. 29, 2019.

194. Paul J. McGeady. "The Harmful Effects of Pornography", *Catholic News Agency*. https://www.catholicnewsagency.com/resources/life-and-family/pornography/the-harmful-effects-of-pornography. Accessed Apr. 29, 2019.

195. Issac Chotiner. "A Sociologist of Religion on Protestants, Porn, and the 'Purity Industrial Complex'" May 3, 2019. *New Yorker*. https://www.newyorker.com/culture/q-and-a/a-sociologist-of-religion-on-protestants-porn-and-the-purity-industrial-complex. Accessed May 19, 2019.

196. Maitland Ward "Maitland Ward: How Porn Saved Me From Hollywood", *Daily Beast*. Jun. 25, 2020. https://www.thedailybeast.com/maitland-ward-how-porn-saved-me-from-hollywood. Accessed Jul. 17, 2020.

197. "Pornography & Public Health Research Summary", *National Center on Sexual Exploitation*. https://endsexualexploitation.org/wp-content/uploads/NCOSE_Jan-2019_Research-Summary_Pornography-PublicHealth_FINAL.pdf. Accessed Dec. 22, 2021.

198. Marcia Segelstein. "How to Protect Your Kids from Pornography"

199. Ibid.

200. Nona Willis Aronowitz. "How to Get an Abortion If You're a Teen", *Teen Vogue*. Jun. 6, 2019. https://www.teenvogue.com/story/how-to-get-an-abortion-if-youre-a-teen. Accessed Jun. 18, 2019.

201. Michael Tennent. "Healthcare 'Death Panels' Alive and Well in Britain", *New American*. Feb. 28, 2011. https://www.thenewamerican.com/world-news/europe/item/8698-healthcare-%E2%80%9Cdeath-panels%E2%80%9D-alive-and-well-in-britain. Accessed Jun. 13, 2019.

202. Steve Doughty. "Top doctor's chilling claim: The NHS kills off 130,000 elderly patients every year", *Daily Mail*. Jun. 19, 2012. https://www.dailymail.co.uk/news/article-2161869/Top-doctors-chilling-claim-The-NHS-kills-130-000-elderly-patients-year.html. Accessed Jun. 12, 2019.

203. Sue Reid. "Now sick babies go on death pathway: Doctor's haunting testimony reveals how children are put on end-of-life plan", *Daily Mail*. Nov. 28, 2012. http://www.dailymail.co.uk/news/article-2240075/Now-sick-babies-death-pathway-Doctors-haunting-testimony-reveals-children-end-life-plan.html#ixzz5qjwYqF15 Original URL has been removed; archive URL: https://web.archive.org/web/20121218104655/http://www.dailymail.co.uk/news/article-2240075/Now-sick-babies-death-pathway-Doctors-haunting-testimony-reveals-children-end-life-plan.html. Accessed Jun. 13, 2019.

204. Terry Wilcox. "The Resurrection of Death Panels", *American Thinker*. Apr. 24, 2019. https://www.americanthinker.com/articles/2019/04/the_resurrection_of_death_panels.html. Accessed Jun. 12, 2019.

205. Adam Goldenberg. "Canada Has Death Panels. And that's a good thing", *Slate*. Oct. 21, 2013. https://slate.com/news-and-politics/2013/10/canada-has-death-panels-and-thats-a-good-thing.html. Accessed Jun. 12, 2019.

206. Susan Donaldson James. "Down Syndrome Births Are Down in U.S." *ABC News*. Nov. 2, 2009. https://abcnews.go.com/Health/w_ParentingResource/down-syndrome-births-drop-us-women-abort/story?id=8960803. Accessed Jun. 12, 2019.

207. "Prenatal Tests Have High Failure Rate, Triggering Abortions", *NBC News*. Dec. 14, 2014. https://www.nbcnews.com/health/womens-health/prenatal-tests-have-high-failure-rate-triggering-abortions-n267301. Accessed Jun. 12, 2019.

208. Julian Quinones, Arijeta Lajka. "'What kind of society do you want to live in?': Inside the country where Down syndrome is disappearing", *CBS News*. Aug. 14, 2017. https://www.cbsnews.com/news/down-syndrome-iceland. Accessed Jun. 13, 2019.

209. Stephen Wynne. "Assisted Suicides Jump 25% In Washington State", *Church Militant*. Aug. 5, 2019. https://www.churchmilitant.com/news/article/assisted-suicides-jump-25-in-washington-state. Accessed Aug. 6, 2019.

210. Courtney Hutchison. "Sterilizing the Sick, Poor to Cut Welfare Costs: North Carolina's History of Eugenics", *ABC News*. Aug. 4, 2011. https://abcnews.go.com/Health/WomensHealth/sterilizing-sick-poor-cut-welfare-costs-north-carolinas/story?id=14093458. Accessed Jun. 12, 2019.

211. "Family Planning Services", *Washington State Department of Social and Health Services*. https://www.dshs.wa.gov/esa/community-services-offices/family-planning-services. Accessed Jun. 13, 2019.

212. Sabrina Gladstone. "Obamacare Mandate: Sterilize 15-Year-Old Girls for Free—Without Parental Consent" *CNS News*. Aug. 10, 2012. https://www.cnsnews.com/news/article/obamacare-mandate-sterilize-15-year-old-girls-free-without-parental-consent. Accessed Dec. 22, 2021.

213. "UK court orders forced abortion for disabled woman", *Catholic News Agency*. Jun. 21, 2019. https://www.catholicnewsagency.com/news/uk-court-orders-forced-abortion-for-disabled-woman-34728. Accessed Jun. 24, 2019.

214. Mike Opelka. "Lesbian Activist's Surprisingly Candid Speech: Gay Marriage Fight Is a 'Lie' to Destroy Marriage", *Yahoo News*. Apr. 29, 2013. https://news.yahoo.com/lesbian-activist-surprisingly-candid-speech-gay-marriage-fight-144222847.html. Accessed May 17, 2019. Audio file URL: http://mpegmedia.abc.net.au/rn/podcast/2012/06/lms_20120611_0905.mp3. Accessed

Jun. 11, 2019.

215. Rosemarie Ho. "Want to Dismantle Capitalism? Abolish the Family", *The Nation*. May 16, 2019. https://www.thenation.com/article/want-to-dismantle-capitalism-abolish-the-family. Accessed Jun. 17, 2019.

216. Martin M. Barillas. "Feminist author: Abortion 'is a form of killing that we need to be able to defend'", *LifeSiteNews*. Jun. 10, 2019. https://www.lifesitenews.com/news/feminist-author-abortion-is-a-form-of-killing-that-we-need-to-be-able-to-defend. Accessed Jun. 18, 2019.

217. Joseph D'Hippolito. "Abortion, Marxism and the 'Progressive' Movement", *The Remnant*. Oct. 31, 2019. https://www.remnantnewspaper.com/web/index.php/fetzen-fliegen/item/4168-abortion-marxism-and-the-progressive-movement. Accessed Jul. 1, 2019.

218. Sharon Smith. "Marxism, Feminism, and Women's Liberation", *SocialistWorker.org*. Jan. 31, 2013. https://socialistworker.org/2013/01/31/marxism-feminism-and-womens-liberation. Accessed Jun. 24, 2019.

219. Jordan Weissmann. "America's Insanely Expensive Child Care Is a Serious Economic Problem", *Slate*. Feb. 11, 2019. https://slate.com/business/2019/02/child-care-day-care-policies-paid-family-maternity-leave-gdp.html. Accessed Jul. 1, 2019.

220. Terence P. Jeffrey. "DOJ: Children Do Not Need—and Have No Right to—Mothers", *CNSNews*. Mar. 3, 2013. http://www.cnsnews.com/news/article/doj-children-do-not-need-and-have-no-right-mothers. Accessed Jan. 16, 2017.

221. Stefano, J.D. Gennarini. "UN Report: 'There Is No Definition of the Family'", *Center for Family and Human Rights*. Jan. 29, 2016. https://c-fam.org/friday_fax/un-report-no-definition-family. Accessed Jun. 24, 2019.

222. Zoltan Istvan. "Should I have let my daughter marry our robot?", *Metro*. Jul. 24, 2019. https://metro.co.uk/2019/07/24/should-i-have-let-my-daughter-marry-our-robot-10361703. Accessed Jul. 26, 2019.

223. Emma Johnson. "Co-parent like a pro", *Wealthysinglemommy.com*. Jul. 5, 2018. https://www.wealthysinglemommy.com/how-to-co-parent-with-an-ex. Accessed Jul. 1, 2019.

224. "About Us", *The New Family* http://thenewfamily.com/about-us. Accessed Jul. 1, 2019.

225. Emma McGowan "7 Alternatives to Traditional Marriage", *Bustle*. Apr. 4, 2017. https://www.bustle.com/p/7-alternatives-to-traditional-marriage-48829. Accessed Jul. 1, 2019.

226. Todd M. Johnson. "Christian Martyrdom: A Global Demographic Assessment", *Notre Dame*. 2012 https://mcgrath.nd.edu/assets/84231/the_demographics_of_christian_martyrdom_todd_johnson.pdf. Accessed Mar. 25, 2019.

227. Stoyan Zaimov. "Christian Churches Deemed 'Illegal Buildings' in China's Mass Demolition Campaign", *Christian Post*. Mar. 27, 2016. https://www.christianpost.com/news/chinas-communist-regime-on-destroy-christian-churches-demolition-campaign.html. Accessed May 8, 2019.

228. Katie Mansfield. "Christian church DESTROYED as Chinese police drag worshippers into street and beat them", *Express*. Jun. 11, 2017. https://www.express.co.uk/news/world/814645/china-church-religion-crackdown-shuangmiao-henan. Accessed 5/8/2019.

229. "Chinese state destroys Christian megachurch as religious crackdown continues", *Christian Today*. Jan. 11, 2018. https://www.christiantoday.com/article/chinese-state-destroys-christian-megachurch-as-religious-crackdown-continues/123441.htm Accessed May 8, 2019.

230. Thomas D. Williams, Ph.D. "Chinese Communists Destroy Catholic Shrines Following Vatican Accord" *Breitbart*. Oct. 26, 2018. https://www.breitbart.com/asia/2018/10/26/chinese-communists-destroy-catholic-shrines-following-vatican-accord. Accessed May 8, 2019.

231. Roni Caryn Rabin. "For Teenagers, the Pleasure of 'Likes'" *New York Times*. Jun. 14, 2016. https://well.blogs.nytimes.com/2016/06/14/for-teenagers-the-pleasure-of-likes. Accessed Jul. 19, 2019.

232. Todd Leopold. "The price of public shaming in the Internet age", *CNN*. Apr. 16, 2015. https://www.cnn.com/2015/04/16/living/feat-public-shaming-ronson/index.html. Accessed Jul. 18, 2019.

233. Caroline Crosson Gilpin. "Are You the Same Person on Social Media as You Are in Real Life?", *New York Times*. May 19, 2017. https://www.nytimes.com/2017/05/09/learning/are-you-the-same-person-on-social-media-as-you-are-in-real-life.html. Accessed Jun. 6, 2019.

234. Mark Milian. "Online personas rarely match real-life behavior, observers say" *Phys.org*. May 14, 2010. https://phys.org/news/2010-05-online-personas-rarely-real-life-behavior.html. Accessed Jun. 6, 2019.

235. Valerie Bauman. "Is America becoming Godless?"

236. "Militant Atheism", *TED*. Feb. 2002. https://www.ted.com/talks/richard_dawkins_on_militant_atheism#t-1678241. Accessed Jul. 19, 2019.

237. Giovanni Dienstmann. "Spirituality vs Religion: The Future of Meaning", *liveanddare.com* (blog) https://liveanddare.com/spirituality-vs-religion. Accessed 7/19/2019.

238. D. Patrick Miller. "The Rapid Dying of Religion & the Rise of a Universal Spirituality", *Elephant Journal*. Feb. 18, 2016. https://www.elephantjournal.com/2016/02/the-rapid-dying-of-religion-the-rise-of-a-universal-spirituality/ Accessed Jul. 19, 2019.

239. Michael Lipka, Claire Gecewicz. "More Americans now say they're spiritual but not religious", *Pew Research*. Sep. 6, 2017. https://www.pewresearch.org/fact-tank/2017/09/06/more-americans-now-say-theyre-spiritual-but-not-religious. Accessed Jul. 19, 2019.

240. Galatians 5:19-21

# A defining moment.
# A simple question.
# A lifetime of answers.

Everyone who serves in the public square is faced with a unique set of challenges. Confronting these trials through the lens of faith presents unique challenges of its own, as well as reasoned solutions.

This is not a partisan manifesto, nor a simple memoir. Rather, *What Are We Looking For?* is a faith-informed examination of public service, written by a man who refused to separate conscience from responsibility.

Available at **CatholicTreehouse**.com

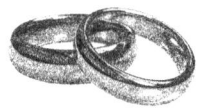

# Discover your purpose. Deepen your faith.
## *Challenge yourself to live like a saint.*

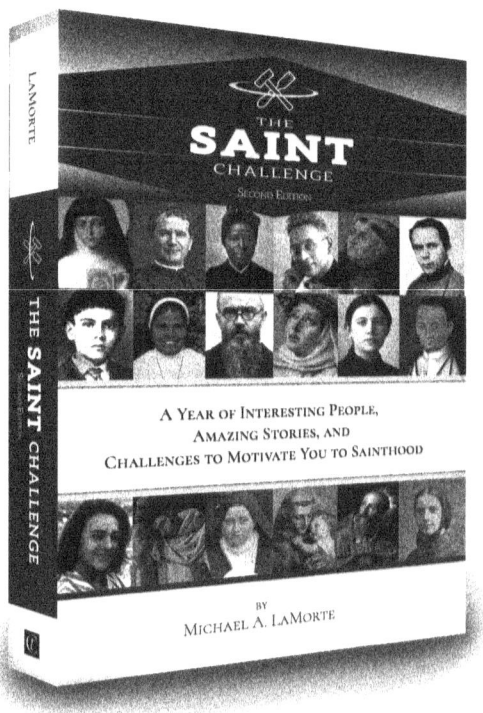

Are you searching for clarity, purpose, and a deeper relationship with Christ? Are you ready to move beyond passive belief and put your faith into action? **Revised and updated for 2026,** *The Saint Challenge* **is more than a saints encyclopedia or a "saint of the day" calendar**—it is a 366-day Catholic devotional designed to transform your spiritual life. Drawing from the powerful witness of the saints, this book invites you to grow in holiness through daily inspiration, reflection, and concrete action.

www.thesaintchallenge.com

www.ingramcontent.com/pod-product-compliance
Lightning Source LLC
Chambersburg PA
CBHW020233130626
46549CB00005B/1863